GW01275839

A VISION OF THE MIDDLE EAST

A Vision of the Middle East
An Intellectual Biography of Albert Hourani

Abdulaziz A. Al-Sudairi

Centre for Lebanese Studies
IBTauris

Published in 1999 by
The Centre for Lebanese Studies, Oxford
in association with
I.B.Tauris & Co Ltd
Victoria House
Bloomsbury Square
London WC1B 4DZ

In the United States of America and Canada distributed by
St Martin's Press
175 Fifth Avenue
New York
NY 10010

Copyright © 1999 by Abdulaziz A. al-Sudairi and The Centre for Lebanese Studies
All rights reserved. Except for brief quotations in a review, this book, or any part thereof, must not be reproduced in any form without permission in writing from the publisher

A full CIP record for this book is available from the British Library
A full CIP record for this book is available from the Library of Congress

ISBN 1-86064-581-X
Library of Congress Catalog card number: available

Copy-edited and laser-set by Oxford Publishing Services
Printed and bound in Great Britain by Biddles Ltd, Book manfactuers

To my daughter, Duna.

Abdulaziz bin Abdulrahman Al-Sudairi was born in Jeddah, Saudi Arabia, in 1959. He earned a BA in economics from the University of Texas in 1983 and an MBA from Texas Christian University in 1985. After working for several years in the field of international business and finance, he joined the Johns Hopkins School of Advanced International Studies (SAIS) where he earned an MA and a Ph.D. and where he is still a Fellow of the Middle East Program.

He has taught and lectured in several American universities and is a member of the Shaybany Society of International Law. Since 1992 he has been a frequent contributor on a wide range of subjects to several Middle Eastern publications, in addition to his work as vice chairman of the Al-Mu'len Company in Jeddah.

Contents

About the Author vi
Glossary viii
Acknowledgements ix
Preface by Roger Owen xi
Introduction 1

1. The Making of a Scholar 15
2. The Ottoman Background of the Modern Middle East 47
3. The Intellectual Origins of Arab Nationalism 77
4. The Problems of Palestine: The Scholar Engagé 106
5. Lebanon: The Pull of the Ancestors 129
6. Conclusion: the Legacy of an Intellectual Mediator 153

References Cited in the Text 181
Interviews 186
A Bibliography of Albert Hourani's Published Works 187
Index 215

Glossary

awqaf	religious endowments
divan	governor's court
imara	princedom
millet	religious community
mutasarrif	provincial governor
mutasarrifiyya	provincial government
Oikoumene	cities and settled agriculture from Atlantic coast of Africa to Pacific coast of Asia
qa'immaqamiyya	administrative district
qabaday's	strong-arm men of the popular quarters
sanjaq	district
shari'a	system of morality and observed codes of Islamic law
silsila	chain of transmission
suq	market
Tanzimat	process of reforms
'ulama	men of religious learning and law
umma	community of believers
watan	love of the homeland
zu'ama	local bosses

Acknowledgements

I was lucky to have received an education from some special teachers and scholars. They gave generously of their time, advice and talent. No student could have wished for a better education. The late Robert E. Osgood introduced me to the study of American foreign policy. From Robert W. Tucker I learned about statecraft and the modern order of nation-states. Frederick L. Holborn was a patient and dedicated teacher; he was always available and worked with me beyond the call of duty. James Piscatori shared his vast knowledge of Islamic history, political philosophy and the Arabian Peninsula. Nicholas Onuf generously agreed to be a member of my examining committee.

A number of scholars — Leila Fawaz, Roger Owen, Bernard Lewis, Charles Issawi, Michael Gilsenan, the late Elie Kedourie — shared with me their knowledge of the work and life of Albert Hourani. I am grateful to them all. The librarians at the Paul H. Nitze School of Advanced International Studies, and the Middle East Institute were patient and considerate with my constant requests and generous with their time and knowledge. Special thanks go to Patricia Lazo of Arlington, Texas, and to Farid Awaness for their steady support and friendship. My writing skills have been much improved thanks to the tutorship of Marion Naifeh. I am also very grateful to Mary Wilson for permission to reproduce her excellent bibliography of Albert Hourani's published works as an appendix to this book.

I owe a special debt to the late Albert Hourani. I regret that this work, begun in his lifetime, was completed a few months after his death. I sincerely want to believe that he would see in this work a fair reflection of his life and intellectual legacy.

Before this book could be published, a number of people contributed a great deal of time and effort into preparing it for publication. I am very grateful to my friend Nabil Al-Khowaiter for his encouragement and support; without his devotion and insistence, this book would not have been published. Nadim Shehadi, director of the Centre for Lebanese Studies in Oxford, adopted the project with great enthusiasm. It is very befitting that this book should be published by an institution towards which Albert Hourani was strongly dedicated and had contributed much to its development. Margaret Owen did a wonderful job in editing my original text and smoothing a scholarly work with its occasional rough points into more palatable literary prose. Talal Fandi meticulously checked my references and quotations. Selina and Jason Cohen did the typesetting with much appreciated skill and patience.

Finally, I want to note the help of my principal advisor and teacher, Fouad Ajami. In completing this intellectual journey, he was always there for me. Whatever difficulties I endured, and there were many along the way, he stood ready to help me. I am grateful to him for the special gift of his friendship, and for what he taught me over the course of the last several years.

Preface

It gives me great pleasure to be able to introduce this study of the intellectual achievement of my teacher, colleague and friend, the late Albert Hourani. I remember Albert's own nicely controlled excitement when he told me that he was being interviewed at length by Dr Al-Sudairi for the project. And I also remember my own excitement when I first got to read the manuscript, in the form of a doctoral dissertation, when I first came to teach at Harvard in 1993.

The book takes as its subject the whole corpus of Albert Hourani's academic writing, beginning with the reports he wrote during the Second World War and ending with his attempt to synthesise a life's work of thinking about the Middle East in his *History of the Arab Peoples*. It treats it in terms of its major fields of inquiry — the Ottoman/Arab relationship, Arab nationalism, Palestine and Lebanon — a structure that allows Dr Al-Sudairi to place each within the context of the particular phases of Hourani's life, from his early interest in nationalism and the status of minorities, through his exploration of the Western impact on Arab thought, to his later concerns with the social history of the Fertile Crescent examined through the prism of the city and its notable inhabitants.

This in turn also allows for some more general, but always

subtle, comments about both Hourani's larger world view and his more direct concerns with the analysis of certain key relationships such as those of power, intermediation and the influence of one mind upon another. Here, Dr Al-Sudairi is also fair to some of Hurani's more trenchant critics, but in a way that brings out the difference between their concerns and his. Whereas they were usually interested — some would say obsessively so — with the ruptures and roughnesses of Arab life, Hourani himself was much more concerned with continuities and the ways in which cultural practices develop over long periods of time.

Nevertheless, this is certainly not a work of hagiography. While Dr Al-Sudairi is clear about the importance of the overall contribution of Hourani's work to the study, as well as the understanding, of the modern Middle East, he is also well able to appreciate some of its limits. It is here that the author's Saudi perspective is particularly significant. Hourani's world is the world of the cities — and their rural hinerlands — of the Fertile Crescent. He recognized the importance of Egypt but clearly did not feel very much at home there. He preferred the hills and mountains of Syria, Lebanon and northern Palestine to the oasis towns of Arabia and the Gulf. And his day to day interest in the contemporary Arab scene had come to an end some years before the era of oil and petro-politics. Those of us who lived closer to Hourani himself were probably dimly aware of this, but lacking Dr Al-Sudairi's fresh perspective, could not always see how such personal predilections affected the larger picture he was working to create.

There are other times, however, when Dr Al-Sudairi seems to stand a little too close to Hourani's own account of his life. You would have had to know Hourani a longer time to realize just how much passion he had spent not just on the cause of an undivided Palestine but also trying to get the British to understand something of the arrogance, as well of the myopia, involved in their exercise of power in post-Second World War Middle East. You would also have to interrogate his views about nationalism a little more than Dr Al-Sudairi does to understand why, for all his support for Arabism in its anti-colonial phase, he knew very well from first hand experience in the early 1940s, that it also contained illiberal tendencies which might lead it in an authoritarian, even self-destructive, direction.

It is an obvious point to make for anyone who lived any length of time in Oxford that Albert Hourani shared not just his ideas but also his life with his students and colleagues in a way that put him apart from any other academic dignitary that we knew. We soon got to learn something of his family history, of his network of cousins and second cousins in the Middle East, Europe and America, of his pleasure that his Woodstock Road garden was adjacent to the famous shed in which T. E. Lawrence dreamed his adolescent dreams. This explains much, but it also hides much. The varied expressions of the liberal world view, the constant concern with questions of religious faith, the intellectual engagement with the varied expressions of Arabism, had a life of their own which we could only discover in his formal lectures and his written work. There is the man, there is his work. Perhaps the most important skill that Dr Al-Sudairi brings to this book is his ability to distinguish between the two, to understands the limits of trying to use the one to explain the other, to see how the work of a great scholar has a shape and an incandescent life all of its own.

Roger Owen
Centre for Middle Eastern Studies, Harvard

Introduction

The Oxford political historian Albert Habib Hourani (1915–93) was undeniably one of the great scholars of the modern Middle East. Between the publication of his first book, *Syria and Lebanon* (1946), and his last, his work of historical synthesis, *A History of the Arab Peoples* (1991), there was nearly a half a century of brilliant academic work. This has left a lasting imprint on the way the modern Arab world, in particular, has come to be studied and understood. The author G. H. Jansen, in his book *Militant Islam* (1979: 9), described Hourani as 'the intellectual godfather to an entire generation — now almost two — of students of, and writers on, the Middle East'. He thereby summed up the great mark that this Anglo-Arab scholar, born in Manchester to a family of Christian Lebanese immigrants, had left on modern Middle Eastern studies.

In a scholarly career of great and unrelenting productivity, Albert Hourani took up some of the large themes of modern Middle Eastern history. These included:

- the making and unmaking of the Ottoman tradition;
- the traffic of ideas between Islam and the West;
- the rise of modern nationalism and its limits;

- the relations between the Western powers and the states of the Middle East;
- the issue of the minorities in the Arab world;
- the nature of social and political power and its bases in Middle Eastern societies;
- the search of Arab intellectuals for viable systems of belief and meaning; and
- the trauma that Arab society experienced after the loss of Palestine in 1948.

Other scholars have taken up some of these questions, but no one else so consistently and thoroughly over so long a period of time.

Not an archival historian but rather a great synthesizer, Hourani dealt with these themes in works of lasting importance and impact. He began with intellectual history — the history of ideas — and eventually worked his way to social history — the history of social elites (the history of notables), of Muslim cities; he began with the study of ideas and ended up borrowing from the field of social anthropology. Perhaps that transition to social history was not as complete and far-reaching as Hourani himself might have wished; nevertheless he spanned both types of history.

A scholar who, in the latter part of his career, avoided political controversy and political commentary, Hourani had an earlier political involvement that makes an intellectual biography of him even more compelling. When the Second World War broke out in 1939, Hourani was offered a position in the Foreign Office Research Department; he was then dispatched to Cairo to work in the office of the British Minister of State where he stayed from 1943 until 1945. After the war ended, he had a particularly important involvement in the Palestinian struggle between Arab and Zionist. Hourani joined

Introduction

the Arab Office, and worked in both London and Jerusalem to promote the cause and articulate the intellectual and moral claims of the Palestinian Arabs. From that effort he emerged chastened when the struggle for Palestine ended in defeat in 1948, determined to stay out of what he described as advocacy and 'policy-oriented research'. Yet, for all his attempts to steer clear of politics, Hourani must be counted one of the two great advocates of Arab nationalism (the Lebanese-born George Antonius, 1891–1942, author of *The Arab Awakening* is the other). Hourani was a distinctly important political and intellectual mediator between the Arab world and the English-speaking world on both sides of the Atlantic.

His British birth and citizenship made England his first and most natural environment. In addition, Hourani did his early political work during what the historian Elizabeth Monroe (1963) described as 'Britain's moment in the Middle East' in the interwar years and the first decade that followed the Second World War. Much of this early intellectual energy and output was dedicated to interpreting the Arab world of his ancestors to Pax Britannica and its officials and publicists. The British imperial administrators helped sponsor the League of Arab States in 1945. Many of them were eager to act as sponsors of Arab nationalism. It was natural for him to concentrate on his home country, then the paramount power in the Middle East. It was only later, in the 1960s, that he would come to know the universities and intellectual life of the United States. By then Pax Britannica had come to an end, and Hourani had set aside involvement in political matters to concentrate on scholarly work.

Timing helped give Hourani the opportunity to leave the imprint he did on Middle Eastern affairs. His scholarly work of the 1950s and 1960s came during the era of decolonization. The West was retreating from the Middle East — at least in its outward colonial form — and there was a search on both sides of the divide for a new pattern of relationship. This gave a scholar of Hourani's temperament and orientation the material and the audience he needed. He would acquire both a scholarly role and a political vocation. Hard as he may have insisted in later years that all his political life lay behind him, it was inevitable that the large themes he dealt with would matter in the political arena.

Hourani's scholarly legacy and the political and intellectual role he came to fill make him a particularly fitting subject for an intellectual biography. The principal aim of the present work is to show how the work of Hourani affords students of the modern Arab world and the Middle East a unique gateway to its emergence and evolution. Hourani stands at the crossroads of great political and scholarly issues. These include:

- Western colonialism and the Arab Muslim response to it;
- Arab nationalism and its modern fate;
- the struggle for Palestine and its meaning for Arabs; and
- the attempt of Arabs exposed to the liberal traditions of the West to reconcile their own indigenous traditions with the ideas that came to them from European sources.

A sustained inquiry into Hourani's life is a rare scholarly venture into the principal debates and developments that attended the making of modern Arab societies. Hourani stood on the shoulders of others: he read widely and was a gifted transmitter of ideas to future scholars. In looking at his work, a good deal of the intellectual landscape of modern Middle Eastern history, and its interpretations, is thus illuminated.

This study is the first full-length inquiry into Hourani's work. No major work of intellectual biography of Hourani has been attempted thus far. Students and admirers of Hourani have written short works of appreciation of his work. Donald Reid (1982: 541–57) wrote a very thorough essay that combines both a long tribute to Albert Hourani's *Arabic Thought in the Liberal Age* and a wider set of reflections on Hourani's general contribution to the field of Middle Eastern studies. The historian Leila Fawaz wrote an essay, 'In Memoriam: Albert Hourani (1915–1993)' after Hourani's death, which acknowledged the debt she and scholars of her generation owed the distinguished historian and teacher (Fawaz 1993: 1–12). Indirectly, scholars with an interest in Hourani could learn something about his family origins and environment from a work published in 1984 by his more politically active younger brother Cecil Hourani entitled *An Unfinished Odyssey: Lebanon and Beyond*. But these short works were limited in scope, sources and intent, and the autobiography of Cecil Hourani could not do justice to the work and legacy of the older Albert. In chronicling his own life, Cecil shed some general light on the world into which Albert Hourani had been born. He provided useful material for those who would carry forward a scholarly examination of Albert Hourani and his work. However, it was left for others to exploit the wider questions of Hourani's scholarly and political temperament and output.

The method used in this inquiry is the method of intellectual biography.

- First and foremost, there is the primary material. This involves a close reading of Hourani's work and a textual analysis of the formidable writings, both published and unpublished, he left us (the works are all cited in the bibliography). Where appropriate, this inquiry traces Hourani's own path. It looks at the scholars Hourani read or was influenced by. The method is carried forward as well. The work of his many disciples and students is

examined so as to situate Hourani himself in a broader intellectual setting.
- A second source of material, and a key to the research, is a number of interviews carried out by this author with Albert Hourani himself, his colleagues, his relatives and his former students, as well as critics. The persons interviewed are listed in the bibliography. The aim was to augment the written record, to draw out both Hourani himself and those who are familiar with his work into an assessment of his contributions.
- The secondary sources are exhaustively consulted and analysed: reviews of his work; writings about him by other scholars.
- Archival research was also undertaken — the files of the Arab Office, and the Foreign Office in London — to document the public role Hourani played both as an advocate of the Arab causes in Palestine and as a researcher for the British government on Middle Eastern affairs.
- As this is a work of intellectual biography, Hourani's output is juxtaposed with the work and contributions of other scholars who worked the same general field and probed the same questions addressed by him.
- This study views Hourani as a liberal historian of Arab and Middle Eastern affairs. He believed in progress, in the self-determination of the Arab world, in the possibility of a convergence between the civilization of the West and that of the Arab world. He believed in a 'social contract' among minorities in a common nation-state. A close look at and analysis of his work is also an inquiry into the working assumptions of liberal historians of nationalisms in the Third World. To reach an appropriate understanding of Hourani's work requires a wider reading of works of political philosophy.

Introduction

This inquiry has sharply drawn limits. It is not, nor is it intended to be, a scrutiny of Albert Hourani's life. It is not a political biography or a psycho-biography of Albert Hourani, the man. There is no intention here to provide either a tale of a life lived or a theory of the motivations that drove Albert Hourani to do what he did and to write on the subjects with which he dealt. The study begins and ends with his intellectual life and the public record of that life.

A second limitation has been already referred to earlier. Because this study is the first of its kind, it more or less stands alone without the benefit of much prior research. A genuinely humble man, Hourani did not encourage, nor was he the subject of, a 'personality cult' that attracted followers and disciples and previous researchers. If future students of the Middle East are encouraged to look deeper into Hourani's work and life, the field will be all the richer for it.

A third constraint has to do with the limitations of Hourani's own studies. He was particularly strong on what he himself described as the 'liberal age' in Arab politics and history: 1798–1948 were the years he specified. By 1798 the impact of the French Revolution of 1789 had begun to be felt in the Arab and Muslim world. That year also marked Napoleon Bonaparte's invasion of Egypt, which shattered the foundations of the old order there and made the region a satellite of Europe. The commerce, the ideas, the authors, and the pilgrims of Europe would descend on the Middle East. The thinkers of the Middle East would come to be awed by Europe and the mystery of its success. The year 1948 marked, of course, the loss of Palestine and the growing popularity of doctrines of fascism and authoritarian nationalism in the Arab world.

These two dates, two historic turning points, serve as markers for Hourani's work. While it is true that he worked on subjects prior to and after these two dates, his work is most at home with history that unfolded between them. The High Middle Ages of Islam were not of particular interest to him. Nor were the radical revolutions that swept the Arab world in the 1960s. His natural themes were the coming of the West, and the responses to that new power. The limitations he imposed on his material are, by necessity, limitations on this study as well.

There are limitations of geographic scope as well. While Hourani wrote on Turkey and here and there paid scattered attention to the Arabian Peninsula and North Africa, he was principally a scholar of the politics of the Fertile Crescent (Syria, Lebanon and Iraq) and Cairo. He was a scholar of urban life, of the cities of the Arab world and of the coastal world of the Levant. In this work, he made no attempt to range far beyond his own concerns. To pick an important example, Hourani tells us very little about the formation of states in the Arabian Peninsula. This was the result of his interest in intellectual history and in Arab liberalism. The states of the Arabian Peninsula and the Gulf produced no thinkers of the Western liberal variety, so Hourani was not drawn to study their political culture.

He also failed to address the impact of oil wealth on state formation and social change in the Arab world. That singular event, encapsulated in the discovery and marketing of oil, and in the spread of the wealth it generated beyond the oil states themselves, was a sea change in Arab society. It is not addressed in Hourani's work despite its great decisive role in the formation of the Arab peoples as a whole: their sense of the possible, their sense of achievement (or lack of it), their role in an industrial world system. In self-defence Hourani could claim that he was not an economic historian (interview with Hourani, Oxford, 22 May 1991), but the changes oil brought about were not just economic changes. They were basic cultural and intellectual changes in the Arab social order.

These limitations acknowledged, a study of Hourani makes critical contributions and adds to our knowledge of key political phenomena and issues in Middle Eastern history. As I will seek to demonstrate in the following chapters, Hourani was the scholar best able to study and portray the Ottoman background of the modern Arab world. A serious reading of his work re-establishes the link between the Ottoman past and the modern Arab world. Nationalist historiography in the Arab world was determined to separate the Arab world from its Ottoman past. Hourani takes issue with this. The Ottoman tradition was home to the Arabs for four centuries. It helped shape relations between ruler and ruled, ideas of citizenship and obedience, basic ideas of what constitutes a political community. Hourani's work, particularly his last big work, *A History of the Arab Peoples*, reintroduces the study of the Ottoman past. Hourani refuses to accept the Arab nationalist idea that these Ottoman centuries were centuries of darkness and retrogression. The popular idea, expounded upon in the works of Arab nationalists such as George Antonius, was to slight that Ottoman background and emphasize the revolt of the Arab against it. This was not the case in Albert Hourani's work. He restored that varied and multi-dimensional background to its rightful place.

Second, from Hourani's work we gain an appreciation of the domestic, internal sources of change in modern Muslim history. While it is true that Hourani began with a strong emphasis on the role of the West in triggering social and political changes in the Muslim world, his basic view began to change with the passage of time. He came to a genuine appreciation of Islam itself, of the ferment within it, of its court life, of its cultural traditions. It is interesting that from dealing with issues of the nineteenth and twentieth centuries (centuries when the West was ascendant in Arab life), Hourani went back to studies of the eighteenth century — a time when the region was more autonomous.

This change reflects his growing conviction that the Muslim reality ought to be studied on its own terms. Though he was not one to slight either the trauma or the gifts that the West brought to the Arab lands and to Islam, he became increasingly curious about the *internal* dynamics of Arab civilization. He worked his way from the outside inwards. In examining his work, one is reintroduced to the coherence of Islamic political society before the coming of the flood from the West.

A third contribution to knowledge concerns the nature of Arab nationalism, its sources, the mix of ideas that made it what it was, the groups that came together to give it its power. Hourani left us a balanced view of Arab nationalism. He saw it rightly as the work of Muslim modernists and Christian Arab secularists. Even when he could not appreciate the fragility of liberal nationalism in the Arab world, his work and the examination of it undertaken in this study help draw a more balanced view of Arab nationalism.

A fourth contribution relates to one of Hourani's great concerns: the struggle for Palestine between the Palestinians and the Zionists. From Hourani's work, and his involvement with Palestine documented here, the performance of the Arab states in that struggle is more adequately understood. Hourani was a visionary when it came to that issue. He understood early on the weakness of the Arab states, their inability to withstand and cope with the Zionist challenge or to come to a realistic assessment of the balance of forces in the international order of the 1940s. Conventional Arab views had emphasized the 'reason' of this or that Arab regime. Hourani, instead, underlined the inability of newly established states, recently granted their independence by reluctant European powers, to understand the ways of Western statecraft. Hourani knew the disparity of power between the Arabs and the Zionists. In one of his remarkable insights about the Arab performance in the war of 1948 and what led up to it, he observed (Hourani 1953: 166): 'The Arab governments made no preparation, either for peace with its concessions, or war with its sacrifices'. A detailed study of Hourani's work on Palestine recovers an important period of Arab history and of the introduction of the Arabs to contemporary international relations.

A further contribution is the rich analysis that Hourani provides of a political society of special importance to him: the Lebanese political order. Hourani was deeply interested in Lebanon and its sectarian pluralism. This was a land of minorities and Hourani had a special talent, it would seem, for understanding plural societies of competing minorities. Scholars of the Arab world often overdo the uniqueness of Lebanon. But Hourani's understanding and exploration of Lebanon throws badly needed light on the politics and political prospects of other plural societies. Syria and Iraq, too, are lands of minorities and distinct communities. From Hourani's work one emerges with a better appreciation of how plural societies create a public order and how that order comes apart. He had a keen eye for how intact communities develop a separate sense of identity in the context of a multi-ethnic state.

Beyond the introduction, the present work consists of five chapters and a concluding chapter. Chapter 1 is a study of the making of this formidable scholar. In it I look at his family background, the Manchester home in which he grew up with its strong memories of Lebanon and commitment to the cause of the Palestinian Arabs. I look at his journey in his mid-twenties to his ancestral land in Lebanon, his political career in the Foreign Office, his advocacy on behalf of the Palestinians and his scholarly life at Oxford interrupted by brief visiting professorships at leading American universities in the 1960s. My principal concern is to show the development of a temperament and a scholarly sensibility rooted both in England and in an Arab world to which Hourani would come to devote himself. As he would become a mediator between England and the Arabs, so it is here that that role begins.

In Chapter 2, I examine Hourani's interest in the modern Middle East's Ottoman background. Though Hourani laid no special claim to being an expert on the Ottoman period and though he came to this subject relatively late in his career, he did in fact leave a substantial intellectual legacy in this area. His analyses of the bases of social and political power in the Ottoman order, of the moral crisis that eventually eroded the legitimacy of Ottoman rule and of the elaboration of authority in Ottoman life are explored in this chapter. With the exception of Morocco and the interior of the Arabian Peninsula, the states of the Arab world had been Ottoman-ruled provinces. The theme here is the connection between the Ottoman past and the Arab present, the continuity between what had been often seen as two separate histories.

The intellectual origins of Arab nationalism are addressed in Chapter 3. This was Hourani's most persistent and important theme, his principal intellectual vocation. The main focus of this chapter is on Hourani's depiction of two streams that went into the making of Arab nationalism — Muslim modernism and the outlook of Christian secularists. Overwhelmingly, Hourani's bet was on a liberal version of Arab nationalism making its way with the help of the West and Arab moderation. The chapter is an attempt to reconcile Hourani's ambivalence as he moves back and forth between a hopeful prognosis for Arab nationalism and a realistic understanding of its limits. These limits include the inability of Arab nationalism to cope with the West, its failure to reconcile the minorities to the new nation-states in the Arab world and its unwillingness to provide for some supranational authority across the boundaries of Arab states. Haunted by a sense of inferiority, Arab nationalism, according to Hourani, vacillated back and forth between rejecting Western political models and uncritically accepting these models. A lingering sense of resentment towards the West underlies this movement across the ideological spectrum that is discernible in the intellectual origins of Arab nationalism.

Chapter 4 is an attempt to examine Hourani's involvement in the struggle for Palestine. This was his big venture into political life. He brought to that issue an intensity that would not be seen in later years, a political zeal and a willingness to engage in political battles. He knew the Arabs' weakness, but persisted in his advocacy. The chapter retraces his attempt to link Pax Britannica's power and prestige in the region with 'fairness' to the Palestinians. Hourani appealed to power, but knew that moral claims could only go so far. He knew that the Arabs were too divided and too politically inexperienced either to check the Zionists or to make England more willing to take their interests into account. This is a study of Hourani's passion and of his morality. It is also a study of the clarity of his thought on Palestinian affairs and of his understanding of the balance of forces, and of the impact that the defeat in Palestine would bring to bear on the future course of Arab politics.

Chapter 5 is a study of Hourani's work on Lebanon, the land of his ancestors, a country he knew well. Its small, intimate politics intrigued him. He knew the traditions of its sects, the political compromises that accounted for its success and the ideologies that led to its breakdown. In this chapter I explore Hourani's understanding of how the political society of

Lebanon emerged from a synthesis between the ideologies of Maronite nationalism based in the heartland of Mount Lebanon and those of Arab nationalism based in the coastal cities of Beirut, Sayda and Tripoli. I look at Hourani's subtle understanding of how a fragile, tenuous conception of Lebanese nationalism spread in a country that became a city-state of sorts — an extension of the city of Beirut and its political culture. Hourani's work shows that Christians did not make Lebanon. The polity that existed until 1975 was a blend of what both the (Maronite) mountain and the (Muslim) coastal cities had created.

Chapter 6 is a brief concluding chapter on Hourani's legacy. In it I look at the themes of his work, at his place in the modern historiography of the Arab world, at the difficulty of being an intellectual mediator between such vastly different worlds with competing interests as the Arab world and the West. In this chapter there is an attempt to come to an assessment of the ambivalence with which Hourani approached the coming into Arab life of the West, of Britain and other powers. It is an appreciation of the lessons the West taught coupled with an understanding of what a relationship of great inequality does to both sides.

1

The Making of a Scholar

The life story of Albert Hourani is best understood as the story of the meeting of two cultures.[1] It is the legacy of the West's encounter with the East. Their amalgam produced a special mind full of contradictions, curiosity, and great imagination. This blend was, in large part, responsible for the fertility of Hourani's mind; it was also the source of a good deal of his intellectual anxiety. Richard Crossman, once Hourani's professor at Oxford and later a member of the Anglo-American Committee of Inquiry on Palestine, wrote in 1946 a fascinating passage which throws a floodlight on Hourani's intellectual outlook:

> The Arab intelligentsia, as I was to find later in Jerusalem, is intensively attractive to the educated Englishman. They have a French elegance of mind and

---

1. Since no work has been done on Hourani's life, a good part of the material in this chapter was based on a series of interviews that the author conducted with Hourani in London and Oxford in May 1991, and a short autobiographical essay supplied to the author by Hourani in April 1991. The latter was published as 'Patterns of the Past' in Naff (1993: 27–56).

expression and are a fascinating mixture of cynical melancholy, shrewd business senses and ingenuous idealism. Inspired by western literature, history and philosophy, yet passionately loyal to their own native culture, they develop the split personality which is almost inevitable for those compelled to live two separate dimensions. Western and Arab thought cannot coalesce either in a single personality or in a single state. They pile up on each other like a stratified rock formation where every now and then the regularity of the pattern had been twisted or broken by some prehistoric convulsion. But because they live in two dimensions, disturbed by the uneasy friction of the eastern and western thoughts and feelings, the educated Arabs are people of immense interest and charm.

(Crossman, 1947: 111)

An appreciation of the intellect of Hourani and of his quest as a historian of the modern Middle East must begin with his family background and early formation. The political historian's themes are best located in the family atmosphere he was born into. We begin there in this chapter and then trace the major phases of his intellectual development.

Albert Hourani was born in Manchester, England, in 1915. A shy and quiet child, he was the fifth of six children — three boys and three girls — of two Lebanese immigrants, Fadlo Hourani and Soumaya Racy. At the end of the seventeenth century, the Hourani family had migrated from the district of Hauran in northern Syria to the village of Marjayoun in southern Lebanon at the present frontiers of Syria, Lebanon and Israel. The late 1860s were the years when European and American missionaries were most active in Lebanon and the

The Making of a Scholar

Houranis were among the first inhabitants of Marjayoun who converted from the Greek Orthodox Church to Protestantism. This conversion of Albert Hourani's grandfather would influence the fortunes of the family for years to come.

Hourani's grandfather had done much to further the spread of Protestantism and when he died the Presbyterian Church, in appreciation of his efforts, decided to sponsor his only son, Fadlo, to enter their newly established Syrian Protestant College (later to become the American University of Beirut). Most graduates of the college, due to their mastery of the English language, went on to work for the British Administration in Egypt or Sudan. Fadlo Hourani, however, chose a different path.

In 1881, at the age of 20, Fadlo Hourani went to Manchester to work for his cousin in the cotton export business. Manchester was a prosperous industrial town. Until the crash of 1929, it was considered one of the world's main centres for cotton and woollen goods. It exported products to the Ottoman Empire and North Africa; merchants from Damascus, Beirut, Baghdad, Cairo, Morocco and Istanbul set up their businesses there. The city was also home to communities of Scots, Syrians, Lebanese, Moroccans and Oriental Jews. Fadlo Hourani became one of many foreigners finding his way in life there.

Upon his arrival, he rented a room where he lived alone. He spent most of his evenings in the public library. He was a well-read man who enjoyed English as well as Arabic literature. He was at ease with English ways but home beckoned and as soon as he had saved enough money, he returned to Marjayoun and built a house for his mother. A few years later, on a second visit to his village, he married Soumaya Racy, whose father was the village Protestant pastor and the headmaster of the

American missionary school in Sayda. Fadlo Hourani had a strong sense of commitment to the land of his birth and during his years in Manchester he travelled 24 times to Marjayoun (Nasir, 1991: 47). He would build a school there, which survives to the present day.

In England, Fadlo Hourani provided his children with a home that mixed the culture of his new world with that of the old. The Middle East and its problems — its way of life as well as its cuisine — were always present in Manchester. We have a portrait of Albert Hourani's family atmosphere, drawn by his brother Cecil:

> Thus to my earliest memories in Manchester there were two faces: the one Near Eastern, Lebanese, full of poetry, politics and business; the other partly Scottish Presbyterian, full of Sunday churchgoing and Sunday school, partly English through an English nanny and a succession of English and Irish cooks and maids.
>
> Nothing epitomized this dichotomy more than the diet on which we were raised: on Saturdays, when my father lunched at home with his Lebanese and Syrian fellow businessmen and clients from abroad, we ate the food of the Lebanese villages — kibbe, and the traditional dish of Saturday, mujaddara, or Esau's pottage: on Sundays there was an English roast, followed by an apple pie or a milk pudding.
>
> (Hourani, 1984: 3)

Fadlo Hourani was a man who saw himself first as Syrian and then — after the establishment of Greater Lebanon — as Lebanese. Yet his life was by no means confined to his Lebanese and Syrian friends and customers. He took an active

The Making of a Scholar

part in the life of Manchester and was a member of the Liberal Party and many of the city's social clubs. In 1946, he became Honorary Consul of Lebanon in Manchester and Northern England. This post gave him an official status that enabled him to participate in the city's official and political life, but somehow this was not enough. Although he considered himself to be a full citizen, Fadlo Hourani could not escape the troubles of an immigrant as he set out to integrate himself and his family into their English society. He was turned down when he took Albert and his elder brother George to apply to one of the best private schools in the area. The headmaster told him that only English boys were accepted. Fadlo Hourani had lived in Manchester for 13 years and considered himself well integrated into the life of the city. Such answers left him feeling humiliated — and challenged. He decided to start a school of his own and founded the Didsbury Preparatory School, named after the section of town where the Houranis lived. The school had only 35 pupils, a third of whom were Lebanese and Syrian, one-third English and the rest Jewish, mostly of Oriental origin.

Albert finished his early schooling at Didsbury and then at the age of 14 was sent to Mill Hill, a public school in London. His father chose it because it was not a Church of England institution, but one that had been founded 150 years earlier for the children of dissenters (Hourani, 1984: 13). Nurtured by a liberal tradition among its headmasters and teachers, Mill Hill had an atmosphere of tolerance and respect for individual freedom. The culture of Mill Hill was to leave a lasting imprint on the mind and sensibility of Albert Hourani.

Scholarly interest in the Middle East was to come during a later period of Albert Hourani's life. From 1933 to 1936 he attended Magdalen College, Oxford and it was during his last year there that he developed an interest in the issues that would henceforth dominate his life. He had been studying philosophy, politics and economics; his readings, standard at Oxford during the 1930s, were heavily concerned with British and European politics, and with the European balance of power. From these issues he found his way to the study of the 'Eastern Question', and to the role of the European powers in the Islamic world.

The culture of Fadlo Hourani's home would feed this scholarly curiosity. In 1936, the noted Middle East historian, Philip Hitti, a friend of young Albert's father, came and stayed with the Houranis for several days. Hitti had just finished his renowned *History of the Arabs*. The future historian would long recall this visit. A Palestinian delegation was next in a long line of Middle Eastern visitors to the Hourani household. The Palestinian group, representing striking workers, came to London and Manchester in 1936. From them Hourani received a detailed report on conditions in Palestine. The year was not an ordinary one: 1936 was the year of the Arab rebellion in Palestine. The long rebellion (1936–39) against the British Mandate and the growing power of the Yishuv (the Jewish community in Palestine) was to shape Albert Hourani's Palestinian sympathies. It was not only his Arab background that pushed him in that direction. There was the generalized academic culture of the time with its leftist orientation and its opposition to British imperialism in all its forms (interview with Hourani, London, 7 May 1991).

During his undergraduate years Hourani studied the English liberal school of thought and was influenced by philosophers such as Locke and Mill. He studied the development leading from Descartes to Kant and learned something of Max Weber's theory of 'ideal types'. By the time he had finished his degree, however, the study of philosophy at Oxford was going in a direction he didn't like. It was moving from a more classical and historical approach towards analytic philosophy and the theory of knowledge (Hourani, 1991e: 2). Thus he decided to pursue a D.Phil. in Middle Eastern history, a field that was hardly developed and in which little teaching was available.

Hourani soon abandoned his dissertation and left England for Lebanon, where he spent two years (1938–39) teaching at the American University of Beirut. He had become attached to the country and in many ways this was a very formative period.[2] It was during these years that he really experienced life in the Middle East for the first time — its culture, passions and rhythms. He was introduced to the ideas of Arab nationalism and to political problems of the Arab world: the question of independence for Syria and Lebanon from French control and the struggle of the Arabs in Palestine.

As an instructor at the American University of Beirut, Hourani met many of the Arab intelligentsia of that period. Two colleagues of his, though, had the most influence on his thinking. One of them was Charles Malik, the newly returned philosopher from Harvard who brought with him a philosophical approach different from the one Hourani had learned at Oxford. The second was Qustantin Zurayq, one of the leading mentors of younger Arab nationalists. Along with the influence of his colleagues and students, two books had a strong impact on him. One was George Antonius's celebrated work *The Arab Awakening*, the other was T. E. Lawrence's *Seven Pillars of Wisdom*. The former was the manifesto of Arab nationalism at the time. Hourani wrote that the book sought to

---

2. For more details, see Chapter 5.

'respond to the challenge of nationalism and give a moral basis to the retention of final power, by establishing a new relationship with the people ruled by Great Britain, and one which offered them the ultimate prospect of independence' (Hourani, 1981: 195). Lawrence's book was the first book to provide him with an insight into Syrian and Arab society. He was moved by the author's prose, by his appreciation of the texture of Syrian and Arab society, by its physical and human setting.[3]

Hourani's years in Beirut were interrupted in 1939 by the outbreak of the Second World War. He returned to London and took a job in the Middle East department, part of a research organization set up by the Royal Institute of International Affairs (RIIA), also known as Chatham House. Arnold Toynbee directed the organization and the scholar H. A. R. Gibb headed its Middle Eastern section. The RIIA was established as a research centre whose main function was to promote better understanding of international affairs in the optimistic hope that such work would help to resolve conflict among nations and prevent the tragedy of war. By that time, Hourani had already read the first volumes of Toynbee's *Study of History* and later read and was influenced by his book *The Western Question in Greece and Turkey*. Hourani considered the latter to be an important analysis of the nature of the relation between great powers and their clients. Hourani read nothing of Gibb but he worked closely with him and was influenced by his deep and impartial evaluation of political movements. The

---

3. As Hourani told the author, the personality of Lawrence inspired him to write what he believed to be his best piece of work, which was an essay on T. E. Lawrence. This appeared in 1983 and was reprinted in his last book, *Islam in European Thought* (1991).

analytical tutoring he received from his reading and contacts would serve him in a more practical setting.

Two years later he was assigned to undertake a mission of inquiry in the Middle East and he remained in Cairo from 1943 to 1945 working in the office of the Minister of State as an assistant to Brigadier I. N. Clayton. There, Hourani gained a better understanding of the politics of some of the Arab countries and met some of the leading personalities such as Glubb Pasha and David Ben Gurion. In addition, he wrote several reports that became the initial drafts of his first three books,[4] books of which he himself grew to be highly critical for two reasons (interview with Hourani, London, 9 May 1991). First, they were too policy-oriented, a style of writing to which he became opposed. It was Gibb's style of 'detached scholarship' that appealed to him and prompted an affectionate essay, 'H. A. R. Gibb: The Vocation of an Orientalist' (Hourani, 1980: 121). Hourani believed that one's own thinking could corrupt analysis. Thus 'policy-oriented writing led to a confusion between two types of discourse, the expository and the moral' (Hourani, 1981: xiii). The second reason why he dismissed his own earlier works is that the point of view is simplistically nationalist. It made the assumption that all Arab countries would unite — an assumption he later found to be totally unacceptable. Despite his self-criticism, however, these works do warrant a closer look. They offer insights into little-explored aspects of Arab society and politics.

---

4. These are *Syria and Lebanon* (1946b); *Great Britain and the Arab World* (1946a); and *Minorities in the Arab World* (1947). In spite of his own view and sense of disappointment, these are books of great originality and indispensable scholarly value.

Minorities in the Arab World was one of these early books. Though seemingly forgotten, it remains, after more than fifty years, the only comprehensive survey and reference work on the position of minorities in the Middle East. In general, most eighteenth- and nineteenth-century European philosophers and historians neglected the subject of minorities, and for his part Hourani did not dwell extensively on the subject. But in the few brief writings he produced, idealistic though they were, we are provided with the starting point for dealing with the subject of minorities in that part of the world. He suggested that the Ottoman Empire — what he called a 'supranational state' — was the focus of loyalty of the different communities, all equal before the Sultan (Hourani, 1947: 121). Here, each community lived separately, in its own section of town; they encountered one another in the marketplace and remained fairly autonomous. But this communal (millet) system could not survive the coming of the age of the nation-state. The position of the minorities became more difficult. Nationalism may have promised assimilation and religious tolerance and secularism, but the reality was more problematic. For a scholar who came from a Christian Arab family, the issue of minorities in the new world of nation-states was close to home. The age of nationalism would be welcomed but its meaning for the minorities would be one to worry about.[5]

The question of minorities was significant but Hourani's attention would turn to more pressing issues. The next phase in Hourani's life was his involvement in the struggle for Palestine. In his last year in Cairo, 1945, he was introduced to

---

5. See 'Race and Religion and Nation State in the Near East' and 'The Concept of Race Relations', in *A Vision of History* (1961: 71–105 and 106–16).

The Making of a Scholar 25

the Palestinian leader Musa Alami. Alami was interested in establishing an organization to counter Zionist propaganda and help promote the Arab cause in Palestine. The Arab Office was founded and Hourani took charge of the Jerusalem branch, becoming the principal writer of most of its publications. He prepared documents submitted by the Arab Office to the 1946 Anglo-American Committee of Inquiry and testified before it as a witness for the Arab side. His political career was short-lived, however; the Arab Office ceased to exist after the loss of Palestine in 1948. Along with it, the saddest and most disappointing chapter of Hourani's life came to a close. It was a period that Hourani had no desire to remember. He wrote:

> I did not like this kind of work, however, and I do not think I was good at it. I did not enjoy the company of politicians and disliked the way in which they thought; I also found it difficult to accept the endless repetitions of political discourse, and the necessity to suppress so many nuances of meaning in order to make a point effectively. I closed this chapter of my life with relief, and have never re-opened it.
> (Hourani, 1991e: 11)

In spite of this, Hourani continued to write about Palestine. It was only in the late 1950s that he quit all writing that was policy-oriented in nature, the only exception being an article that he wrote after the 1967 war entitled 'Palestine and Israel'.[6] Indeed, after the fiasco of 1948, Hourani found it more difficult to believe in any kind of united and effective Arab action: all of his dreams were shattered. He remained sceptical even as 'Abd

---

6. For more details, see Chapter 4.

al-Nasir rose and many others were convinced the Arab world was on the verge of unity. He did not believe much would come out of such a union (interview with Hourani, London, 9 May 1991).

There was, in 1948, a call back to academic life and its serenity, back to his old college, Magdalen, in Oxford, where he would begin a 30-year period of deep involvement in the life and affairs of the university. It was a period of expansion of 'oriental studies' in British academic institutions. Oxford was given a fund by the government for that purpose and Hourani was appointed to one of the newly created jobs. Hourani's wartime colleague H. A. R. Gibb headed the Faculty of Oriental Studies and very much wanted departments of social science and humanities to expand their range far beyond the study of British and Western subjects. At a time when most departments had shown little interest in such an undertaking, Gibb decided to establish a nucleus of specialists in different subjects within the faculty of oriental studies who in turn would try to reach other faculties of the university. Hourani was to be the modern historian of this group. He devoted all his time and energy to his students. He had taught undergraduates before the war at the American University of Beirut, but he felt more at home working with graduate students. Working in the open door tradition of Oxford, he took great satisfaction in guiding his students through their full course of graduate study. Among his first students were Jamal Muhammad Ahmed, a superb Sudanese scholar who later became a foreign minister of his country, and André Raymond, who become one of the most distinguished Middle Eastern historians of his generation.

The 1950s were a period of great change in Hourani's intellectual interests as well as his personal life. He was married in 1955 to Odile Wegg-Prosser, who gave him, in 1956, his only daughter, Susanna, a teacher of science at Surrey University and the mother of Hourani's only grandchild. For a religious man, one of the most important changes in his personal life was his conversion from Protestantism to Catholicism. It might be natural to think such a change came as a result of his marriage to a Catholic woman, but it did not; according to fellow historian Charles Issawi, the idea of converting to Catholicism had its appeal to Hourani long before his marriage.[7] He was attracted by the more hierarchical structure as well as by the cultural and spiritual aesthetic of the Catholic Church. He was fascinated by Catholicism's comprehensiveness, which encompassed many aspects of life and social activities. For him, Catholicism had a great level of certainty on such fundamental questions as individual salvation and the means of attaining it. Although the conversion proved to be an important sustaining force in his life, it did not appear significantly to recast his scholarly writing and outlook.

On the intellectual side, Hourani decided he would no longer write with a policy-oriented approach but would look to 'produce something more in conformity with an ideal of detached scholarship directed towards an understanding of the past' (unpublished biographical essay, 14). In this he was faced with several obstacles: he was neither trained as an orientalist nor was he prepared to be a historian of classical Islam. Moreover, at that time the academic study of the modern Middle East in both Britain and the United States was just developing;

---

7. Interview with Charles Issawi, Princeton, NJ, 12 June 1991. Issawi told the author that ten years before his conversion, he had made and won a 50-dollar bet with Hourani's older brother, George, with respect to Hourani's desire to convert.

Hourani was the second person in Great Britain to be appointed to teach Middle Eastern history. Thus he had to start searching for his own foundations. Gibb provided a springboard. He had propounded a method for understanding the inner history of Islamic civilization that was based on the *silsila*, or chain of *'ulama* (men of religious learning and law). According to this approach, learning was passed from one generation to another through a series of thinkers, each building on the ideas of the preceding one. Hence the continuity of a cultural tradition. Hourani would later apply this method to his own work. He also read some of the work of European travellers and searched rather aimlessly in the Public Record Office without quite knowing what he was looking for. His study and queries inevitably led to a good deal of analytical probing.

During the 1950s, Hourani spent most of his time trying to write a book about the Arab provinces of the Ottoman Empire in the nineteenth century. The work was never completed, never saw the light of day and was only kept in a box.[8] The RIIA commissioned Hourani to write this work as a continuation of the series on *Islamic Society and the West*, which Harold Bowen and H. A. R. Gibb had started and which was based on Toynbee's analyses of the impact of one rising civilization upon another that was in decline. As Hourani was writing his work, he became more and more discontented with this framework of ideas. In long critiques of Toynbee's vision of history, which he wrote in 1955, Hourani found Toynbee's

---

8. In an interview in London on 10 May 1992, Hourani told the author that most of the material on the Ottoman Empire in *History of the Arab Peoples* was drawn from his never completed work on that subject.

ideas to be 'moral ones', a concept that had influenced his own earlier work ('A Vision of History: An Examination of Professor Toynbee's Ideas', in Hourani, 1961: 11). Hourani implied that Toynbee reduced the study of history to the analysis of civilizations as the ultimate unit of study, and neglected the role of man in history. 'How far is he [man] free in history and, in so far as history obeys laws, what is the human basis of those laws?' (Hourani, 1961: 15). In his autobiographical essay he wrote:

> Was 'Islamic society' so stagnant, was it not changing at its own pace and in its own way? Was 'western civilization' likely to absorb all others, and create a new world unified not only at the level of techniques for the control of nature but at those of the organization of society and beliefs about the nature of the universe?
> (Hourani, 1991e: 16)

But it was not easy for Hourani to free himself from Toynbee's influence. His next project, *Arabic Thought in the Liberal Age*, a synthesis of essays he started in 1956 and which appeared in 1962, was a study of the effects of one civilization on another, precisely what Toynbee would have done. As a historian of ideas, his interest in starting such a book — which turned out to be his most influential — sprang from three elements. First, there was his interest in the history of thought for its own sake, 'in taking an idea, showing how it grew, was linked with others within a system, answered certain questions and gave rise to others' (Hourani, 1981: xiv). Second, was a 'concern with the problem of belief in the modern world: with the relationship and tension between the attempts of the individual mind and conscience to articulate the truth, and the great cumulative traditions of human thought and spirituality' (Hourani, 1981: xv). And, finally, there was his reading of Edmund Wilson's *To the Finland Station*, a book that probed the development of ideas and the way in which man can use ideas to change his world (interview with Hourani, Washington, DC, 10 May 1989).

The material of *Arabic Thought* demonstrated how a dozen or so Muslim and Christian Arab authors rooted in the intellectual traditions of their land responded to the social and political power of the nineteenth century. The underlying hypotheses of the work — as Donald Reid put it in a review of Hourani's work — is 'that ideas can largely determine the direction of social and political change, that popularizing intellectuals play central roles in their societies, that Western contact awakened a rather stagnant Middle East, and that liberal nationalism was the most potent force of the age' (Reid, 1982: 547).

Reid was most successful in showing the degree of importance of *Arabic Thought* and the magnitude of its influence on the writing of many of Hourani's contemporaries and the younger generation of scholars of Middle Eastern studies.[9] It is

---

9. Reid has collected some of the many written testimonials in appreciation of Hourani's work. For example, Hisham Sharabi writes: 'I wish to acknowledge my indebtedness to Albert Hourani, whose pioneering work, *Arabic Thought in the Liberal Age, 1789–1939*, is an indispensable reference to any study of modern Arab intellectual history.' C. Ernest Dawn writes: 'The longstanding need for a systematic and comprehensive treatment of modern Arab intellectual history has now been satisfied by Albert H. Hourani's masterful *Arabic Thought in the Liberal Age*.' 'For the modern period,' writes Charles Wendell, 'the chief secondary source of inspiration has been Albert Hourani's *Arabic Thought in the Liberal Age*' (Reid, 1982: 549–50).

safe to say that an entire generation of scholars in the field chose their dissertation topics — as well as topics for other studies — from this book. As could be expected, the book had less influence on those who were well established in the field than it did on the younger generation of scholars. Yet, even the older scholarly establishment found in it ample material for controversy and study.[10]

Most of Hourani's critics and reviewers seem to agree that *Arabic Thought in the Liberal Age* had its shortcomings. On more than one occasion, Hourani recognized that there had been no 'liberal age',[11] and that the book had overestimated the power of ideas as the prime factor of change in a society. He recognized that it ignored political and sociological changes that were taking place within Arab societies, and that his synthesis failed to consider those thinkers who worked within the Islamic traditions and whose ideas were not formed in response to the infringing power of the West. Of *Arabic Thought* he was to write:

> It lays its main emphasis on those writers who accepted ideas from Europe more or less willingly, and sometimes eagerly, but does not give due attention to those who

---

10. For example, Hourani's essay on Afghani induced and contributed to the ongoing debate between two of the most eminent scholars of the Middle East, Elie Kedourie and Nikki Keddie. See Kedourie (1966: 3); Keddie (1968: 37 and 1972). See Albert Hourani's review of Keddie's *An Islamic Response to Imperialism* (1968) in *International Journal of Middle East Studies* (1, 1970: 90–1).

11. See Introduction to *The Emergence of the Modern Middle East* (Hourani, 1981) and Preface to the 1983 edition of *Arabic Thought in the Liberal Age, 1789–1939* (Hourani, 1962).

rejected them, or at least accepted them partially and slowly by a cautious adaptation of their own inherited ways of thought, and it does not address the questions why, in what ways, and to what extent the ideas of these individual writers were communicated to sections of society, and for what purposes they were used. It ignores the changes in collective 'mentalities', habits of thought deeply rooted in established ways of life in common.

(Hourani, 1991e: 18)

A historian with a conservative mind like Elie Kedourie argued that the liberal-minded Hourani had relied on literary sources and neglected the archival ones (interview with Elie Kedourie, Washington, DC, 17 February 1992; see also Reid, 1982: 551). Hourani took the words of the liberal thinkers he studied at face value; he assumed their text alone was enough. With hindsight, Hourani (1980a: 195) came to recognize the deficiency of his method.[12] His future work — particularly his definitive and substantial *A History of the Arab Peoples* — was to show that he had come to appreciate the risks of writing intellectual history in isolation from its social and political environment. Intellectuals can write but if their work is to have meaning it must connect with social and political reality. A quarter-century separated Hourani's intellectual history *Arabic Thought in the Liberal Age* from the bigger and more ambitious book, and the result is infinitely richer and more rewarding. The whole society is illuminated in *A History of the Arab*

---

12. Here, Hourani wrote thoughtfully about the importance of the use of archival sources for different periods of Middle East history.

Peoples: the rulers and the ruled, the military, the guilds, the world of the cities, the intellectual traditions. Intellectual history becomes just a part of a broader societal framework. Thus the work is more vivid and anchored in social and political realities (Hourani, 1991a and 1991b).

Hourani was the sort of man who was very conscious of things around him: it was very important for him to stay in touch. He had unlimited energy in keeping up with all news of his friends, colleagues and even adversaries. Hardly a day passed by without him making many phone calls and writing letters to friends all over the world. Seldom could one sit with him without hearing him say, 'I have learned this from this or that person. I have learned this from this book or that idea.' He was always learning and looking for new ideas and it was rather fascinating that a man of his age and achievements was capable of constant change. As the prominent historian Bernard Lewis put it during an interview in Washington, DC on 10 September 1991: 'Hourani was a historian of ideas who now became a historian of society.' This major change from intellectual history to social history was the product of two intense intellectual exposures. These were his visit in 1962 to the University of Chicago where he had his first close look at the study of social sciences and anthropology and his contact with the French school of thought named after the French periodical *Annales*. The French historians who were associated with this school reinforced questions derived from Marxism; they were concerned about the deeper structures of society and the dynamics of change in social groups.

> Now we are in the age of 'social history', the study of economic relationships and the deep structures of society, and of changes in them, within a framework of

ideas derived from Marxism, or from the historians of the *Annales* school, or from a mixture of the two. At its most interesting, this becomes a study of the relationships between power and wealth, how each of them affects the other: in other words, of 'political economy', to use an old word which in recent years has been given a new usage.

(Hourani, 1991c: 134–5)[13]

Writings like Jacques Berque's *Egypt: Imperialism and Revolution* sharpened Hourani's awareness of the significance of the change that elites and reforming rulers tried to force upon traditional societies (see Hourani, 1991b: 131). In his social approach to history, Berque was concerned with the problem of alienation, something that has always persisted, but never been answered, in most of Hourani's writing:

How can men and women repossess a world which has grown alien to them, and do so without losing their authenticity? How can they avoid the two dangers of a stagnant reassertion of an identity inherited from the past, and a cosmopolitan and featureless modernity?

(Hourani, 1991b: 129)

Of all the *Annales* school writers it was André Raymond, one of Hourani's first students at Oxford, who gave him great insight into social structure in the 'Islamic city'. What was the nature of the changing relationship between the urban elites of

---

13. In May 1991, Hourani provided the author with a preliminary draft.

merchants and the artisans? In other words, how was wealth in the city related to political power, and what was the nature of the relationship between the city and the countryside? Moreover:

> Raymond is not willing to accept the theory that, in the absence of formal institutions of municipal self-government, Muslim cities were not cities in the full sense. To judge them in this way, by the absence of something which existed in European cities, is to obscure the reality. They had their own ways of regulating their life in common; apart from occasional violence among the ruling groups and the soldiers, the great cities were places of good order and security. ... A reader of [Raymond's] books will take away with him the impression of a historian who has not only studied documents, but who has walked the streets of the cities using all his senses, and above all the sense of sight.
> (Hourani, 1991d: 14)[14]

Raymond's thought presented Hourani with a lasting theme most obviously first applied in his essay 'The Islamic City', then in *A History of the Arab Peoples*. Islamic cities had their own distinct character and, in their respective settings, they played a more important role in history than did their European counterparts. Middle Eastern culture was a predominantly urban one and cities were the centres of political power, wealth and religious learning. Over the centuries, the 'Islamic

---

14. Hourani gave the author a preliminary copy in May 1991.

city' and its urban life had unified and preserved 'Islamic civilization'. Such themes remained with Hourani to be expanded and reintroduced over the course of many years, but his train of thought was constantly interrupted by larger events.

Hourani spent the academic year of 1956–57 as a visiting professor at the American University of Beirut. But this time again political trouble intruded; the Suez crisis erupted into a full-scale war. He was a witness to a great historic turning point in the traffic between the Arab world and the West (see 'A Moment of Change: The Crisis of 1956', in Hourani, 1961: 117–44). He was to describe the change as a moment 'in which the complex relation of world powers, regional powers and local movements become clear, and are subtly changed' (Hourani, 1991e: 19). The Suez crisis marked the last episode of the European adventure into the lands of the Middle East, and put an end to British prominence in this part of the world.

At the end of the crisis, Hourani returned to Oxford to become the director of the newly created Middle East Centre at St Antony's College, a position he took after Gibb's departure to Harvard to become a professor and director of its Middle East Centre. As he put it, the move from his old college, Magdalen, to the new college of St Antony's was the most creative period of his life. St Antony's, a graduate college whose existence was made possible by an endowment given by a Frenchman who had made his fortune in the British colony of Aden, was different from any other college at Oxford. Here, graduate work was less isolated and more interactive; students and scholars in different but related fields could work together and share a common framework of categories and methodology. The founders of the college believed that it was essential for Oxford to begin recognizing the importance of the study of regions other than Europe and North America. Hourani's time at the Middle East Centre was full of work, joy and excitement.

> I was fortunate enough to find congenial colleagues, among whom I should mention Elizabeth Monroe, the most helpful and unselfish of colleagues, and whose main book, *Britain's Moment in the Middle East*, will continue to be read for its insight into the way in which British policy was formulated and carried out in the later imperial age. I also remember with affection and gratitude the many dozens of graduate students who came to the College, attended seminars, and in some cases wrote dissertations under my supervision; students came more from the United States, Germany and the Middle East than from Great Britain, and in the earlier years it was even possible to pay for them. It was exciting to create ways of teaching and interacting with them, in a university where graduate studies had been slow to develop. We had a permanent seminar where colleagues as well as students met to exchange ideas; apart from that, I tried as far as I could to keep my door open.
>
> (Hourani, 1991e: 19–20)

There was also the recommendation of the Hayter Committee of 1962 to reaffirm what had already started in St Antony's. The British government commissioned the committee to examine the future of African, Asian, and Russian and Slavonic studies. It recommended that the government should give financial help to expand these studies, but in certain directions and in a limited number of universities, Oxford to be among them. As Hourani wrote in 'H. A. R. Gibb: The Vocation of an Orientalist' (Hourani, 1980: 129), 'Departments of history and social sciences should be encouraged to give a larger place to the history and societies of the world beyond Europe, that steps should be taken to train the "new kind of academic amphibian".' Both the directorship of the Middle East Centre at Oxford and the implementation of the recommendation of the Hayter Committee drew Hourani closer and closer to university politics and administration. He became deeply interested in Oxford University as an institution, an interest that was so solid that in the 1960s he refused many excellent offers by Harvard and other prestigious academic institutions in the United States in which he had worked as a visiting professor. In 1962 and 1963 he was invited to teach at the University of Chicago, later becoming a visiting scholar twice at the University of Pennsylvania, twice at Harvard, and once at Dartmouth College. Although Hourani chose to return to Oxford, he still expressed a sense of joy and lasting benefit when he talked about his experience in America as 'periods of productive happiness' (Hourani, 1991e: 22). There was the joy of working in the great American libraries. There was also the feeling of being a member of a history department and finding that fellow historians in other parts of the world took what he was writing seriously. It was quite inspiring and challenging to teach American graduate students who had an unlimited appetite for learning. Chicago gave him his first contact with social anthropology and its application to history, yet it was Harvard that made the most serious impact on him. As Harvard in 1972 did not make an appointment after the retirement of Gibb whose health was deteriorating, Hourani — although his visiting professorship was over — continued to supervise graduate students in Middle Eastern history. Many of Hourani's friends feel that Harvard exploited him. But this didn't seem to matter to him. He was enjoying what he was doing and could have stayed there had he wanted. But his loyalty belonged on the other side of the Atlantic, back at Oxford: 'life is full of doors opening into rooms one has not entered' (Hourani, 1991e: 22).

Inspired by his American experience and by the earlier experience of the *Annales* school, Hourani was to become less and less interested in the form of political history he once wrote, a history that focused on relations between the Arab nationalist movement and the European powers. He grew less interested as well in the intellectual history that had always held him. Gradually he was being pulled into social history. Thus, Hourani entered what he called the years of uncertainty (1965 to 1980). After finishing his *Arabic Thought in the Liberal Age*, he again immersed himself in his major project on Arab provinces of the Ottoman Empire, but he was once again unable to finish it. He spent those years reading new books and wrote many of his influential essays in which such ideas were reflected.

The essay was to be Hourani's genre during this period. In 1968 he wrote what many scholars believe to be his definitive and most important single essay, 'Ottoman Reform and the Politics of Notables' (reprinted in Hourani, 1981: 36–66). The cities of the Ottoman world had witnessed great upheaval in the nineteenth century. An old order had begun to come apart. The indirect method of control so characteristic of Ottoman administration was being abandoned. The essay probed the phenomenon of this urban disorder and rooted it in the growing tension between a centralizing bureaucracy and older methods of social control. The essay was an inspiration for many dissertations. The idea of 'a specific politics of notables' has been accepted and used by a considerable number of scholars in the field (for example, see Khoury, 1983).

One scholar in particular became a source of deep inspiration to Hourani himself: the historian Marshall Hodgson of the University of Chicago (interview with Hourani, London, 6 May 1991). In Hodgson's *The Venture of Islam* he was to find many appealing ideas (see 'Marshall Hodgson and the Venture of Islam', in Hourani, 1991b: 79–81). It was the reading of this book that brought Hourani to a deeper understanding of the ideas of the great Muslim philosopher of history, Ibn Khaldun, on the causes of stability and change. From Hodgson's work, Hourani was to perceive the futility of dwelling on the terms of the relationship between the Arab world and the West. He grew more interested in the internal dynamics of Islamic history; he came to appreciate that societies change at their own pace and within their own available resources. Hodgson's inspiration helped him break from Toynbee's emphasis on 'civilizational units' as the basic categories of analysis. For Hodgson, the intelligible unit historians had to study was the *oikoumene*, the whole world of cities and settled agriculture stretching from the Atlantic coast of Africa to the Pacific coast of Asia. The area stretching from the Nile to the Oxus — a centre of culture and power from the early ages until the early modern period — is only part of the *oikoumene*. From Hodgson's ideas, Hourani deduced that Islam had not started 'something completely new', but had given a 'new form and direction' to existing civilizations ('Marshall Hodgson and the Venture of Islam', in Hourani, 1991b: 79–80).

By itself Islam was not sufficient to explain the communal life of the social structure of medieval Cairo or Baghdad. Attention must also be paid to the social relationships created by patterns and methods of production and exchange, to the relationship between military power and other social forces and, finally, to the general restraints of geographic position and limited resources within which all human societies live.[15]

In 1971, Hourani gave up his post as the director of the Middle East Centre at Oxford and went to Harvard to spend one year as a visiting professor. When he returned to Oxford he continued to carry a full load of teaching and administrative work. But the 1970s were years of bad health for Hourani; he came to talk of his heart attack in 1980 with sorrow and regret. The deterioration of his health gave him a feeling of weakness and exhaustion, an inability to do all he wanted to do. For him a choice had to be made. In 1979 the old master decided to retire, three years before the mandatory age of retirement. Soon he was to discover that retirement was a sort of psychological trauma. Oxford was an intimate, small place, a university town where people lived close together and everyone knew what everyone else was doing. A splendid working environment, Oxford proved a difficult place of retirement. Hourani was cut off from the life of the university. Five years after his retirement he left Oxford for London. He chose a quiet neighbourhood in north London, not too far from the University of London's School of Oriental and African Studies. A visitor to his house could not escape Hourani's own portrayal of the lifestyle of his old mentor in 'H. A. R. Gibb: The Vocation of an Orientalist' (in Hourani, 1980: 111), for it describes his own. 'He had no concern for the elegance of his possessions: he and his wife lived in an orderly, neat, and comfortable way, his books, his furniture and his houses were well cared for but were for use rather than display.'

---

15. Hourani and Samuel Stern organized a conference in 1969 to discuss the specific nature of the 'Islamic City' that Europeans such as Louis Massignon and other French scholars had put forward (see Hourani, 1970).

His was to prove an active and productive retirement. He found the time long needed for sustained research and writing.[16] A television series, *The Arabs*, on which he worked as a consultant, helped him to map out *A History of the Arab Peoples*, a work that started with the rise of Islam and ended at the present time.

This work can be conceived to be the culmination of Hourani's learning and a reflection of the kind of history — social history — that he had long wanted to write. In *A History of the Arab Peoples*, Hourani left his readers with four principal themes. First, Islam is the source of a persistent culture, which the Arabic language of the Qur'an has preserved and articulated. Second, Hourani attempted to show the common factors of unity and disunity in different regions of the Arab world. The geographical position and the physical environment varied between those Arab countries that lay on the Mediterranean coast and those on the Indian Ocean. Apparently, this particular point presented Hourani with an enigma when trying to incorporate the Gulf or the Maghrib into the same framework of analysis as that of the Fertile Crescent countries, which he knew best and where he placed most of the emphasis. Third, throughout his book he aimed to show the dynamic of the complex relationship between the rulers, urban elites and the common people. He was also successful in tracing the lines of the changing alliances of interests between the first two. These are:

---

16. Aside from his book *Syria and Lebanon*, which he wrote in 1946, and until the appearance of *History of the Arab Peoples*, which he wrote in 1991, all he was able to produce was in the form of relatively short but influential essays.

the rulers defending the fabric of civilized urban life, production and exchange, in return for obedience, financial contributions and the legitimacy which the elite could confer through its control of minds, whether expressed in Islamic terms or, in the modern period, through those of 'Arabism'.

(Hourani, 1991e: 31)

Finally, Hourani tried to avoid what he always called the 'danger of writing the history of societies', and ignoring the role of the individual in historical progress, that is, the tendency to 'reduce the lives of individual human beings to movements of classes or other collectivities' (Hourani, 1991c: 26). According to Hourani, the missing point might be that the 'interaction of Power and Wealth creates the "political economy" of a society, but there is also a "moral economy", formed by the interaction of both of them with Truth' (Hourani, 1991e: 31).

How, then, would Hourani have liked future generations of historians to write the history of the modern Middle East? Obviously, 'social history', along the same lines as the *Annales* school, would be his answer. But the role of individuals (the power of ideas) must never be neglected. In writing the history of the Middle East, a historian needs to pay more attention to the centuries of Ottoman rule, since what happened in that region was nothing other than the slow transformation of the old and complex system of the Ottoman government (Hourani, 1991c: 9). Hourani believed one of the greatest tasks before historians is to investigate the Ottoman archives, not only in Istanbul, but also in the provincial cities or wherever direct Ottoman rule existed. In addition to archives, they should be able to utilize the studies of coins, cities, buildings, maps and plans ('Present State of Islamic and Middle Eastern Historiography', in Hourani, 1980: 167–72).

Historians must not look at historical developments of the modern Middle East as a mere reaction to European power and influence, as he and Gibb had done. They should look further and deeper into the internal developments within the society, to popular social movements and to those thinkers who did not accept the ideas of the West.[17] Thus,

> in trying to explain the history of the Middle East in modern times we should always be aware of two interlocking rhythms of change: that which reforming governments and thinkers, and external forces, tried to impose upon society, and that which a great stable society with a long and continuous tradition of thought and of life in common was producing from within itself, partly by its own internal movement and partly in reaction to forces coming from outside.
> (Hourani, 1991c: 10)

We must also, he argued, beware of those movements of thought that might have accepted or responded to the infringing power of the West, yet *did not* completely break with the past. It was only an attempt on their part to adapt traditional ways of thought to the demands of rapidly changing societies in a new world.

---

17. For examples of such thinkers and popular movements, see 'Sufism and Modern Islam: Mawlana Khalid and the Naqshbandi Order,' and 'Sufism and Modern Islam: Rashid Rida,' in Hourani, 1981: 75–89 and 90–102.

Those who are writing the history of the Middle East must not look at the Islamic state as something produced by internal processes, while ignoring the rule of pre-Islamic heritage and culture such as the Byzantines and Sasanians ('Present State of Islamic and Middle Eastern Historiography', in Hourani, 1980: 182). The danger in doing so would be the perception of Islam as the main vehicle towards the understanding of all social and historical developments; Islam can surely help to interpret part of the story but it cannot explain it all.

> Ought we, for example, to explain that special balance between military elite and bourgeoisie, between authority and rebellion, by the Islamic theory of politics? It is tempting to do so but it may be dangerous. We must at least ask whether there are not other explanations, economic or political: the conditions in which settled agriculture was carried on in the Middle East, the need for irrigation and urban capital; the pressure of Arab and Turkish nomads on the countryside and the trade-routes; and so on.
> ('The Islamic City,' in Hourani, 1981: 33–34)

Hourani strongly believed that the writing of the history of the Middle East would be feeble and incomplete unless the work of American and European scholars was supplemented by the efforts of indigenous scholars who were born and raised in that part of the world. They have a better feel for the land and the texture of its life, and have family and cultural ties that foreign scholars do not have. Hourani recognized that most of these Arab scholars work under great difficulties and most of them end up staying in or emigrating to Europe and America. Still, for Hourani the fact remained that 'the writing of history is an act of self-reflection of a collective consciousness, a community taking stock of its own past and what has made it what it is, creating its own principles of emphasis and categories of explanation.[18]

---

18. This is the final sentence in Hourani's autobiographical essay (Hourani, 1991e: 34). He felt so strongly about it that he made clear to this author that he wanted this statement quoted (interview with Hourani, London, 15 May 1991).

2

The Ottoman Background of the Modern Middle East

In *A History of the Arab Peoples*, Hourani would like his readers to perceive all of his works as merely the study of the history of sociological development in Arab societies. But this does not tell the whole story. His work on the Arab provinces of the Ottoman Empire gives us great insight into the origins of factors (whether political, economic or sociological) that led, or contributed, to the birth of the modern Arab states. His narrative begins with the seventeenth century and the Arab region under Ottoman control, and ends in the 1950s with the last episode of the European powers as major players in the Middle East. Hourani's main focus was the study of urban life in the great cities of the Fertile Crescent and, to some extent, Cairo, rather than an extensive analysis of the region under Ottoman control.[1] Nevertheless his analysis provides clues to the elusive answers to some of the more puzzling questions

---

1. In this chapter the phrases 'Ottoman rule' or 'Ottoman control' will be used interchangeably and will always refer to the Ottoman rule over the Arab provinces of the empire.

scholars of the region have faced. Here our main concern is to examine Hourani's studies of Arab societies under Ottoman rule, and critically to trace his lines of analysis to the texture of the sociopolitical fabric of such societies.

Hourani's excellent work on this subject has yet to be adequately acknowledged. We are by no means trying to suggest that his work in this area was undermined; rather it was never fully recognized. It is possible to point to several reasons for this. First, until the appearance of *A History of the Arab Peoples*, Hourani had not produced any comprehensive account (see Hourani, 1991a: 209–64).[2] He had instead produced a series of scattered, sporadic essays.[3] Second, he himself was not convinced that he did much to explain the Ottoman age. Third, with few exceptions (Hourani; Gibb and Bowen, 1957; and Raymond, 1985), a significant number of contemporary scholars believe that undue weight need not be assigned to the five-century long Ottoman heritage and rule, that an understanding of that age adds little to our under-

---

2. He did attempt, in the 1950s, to write a book about the Arab provinces of the Ottoman Empire, which was to be a continuation of the series launched by Gibb and Bowen. He never finished it.
3. Of Hourani's most important analyses of the Arab provinces of the Ottoman Empire, I would rank them in order of importance as follows. First, 'Ottoman Reform and the Politics of Notables' (in Hourani, 1981: 36–65); second, 'The Islamic City' (in Hourani, 1981: 19–35); third, 'The Ottoman Background of the Modern Middle East (in Hourani, 1981: 1–18); fourth, 'The Fertile Crescent in the Eighteenth Century' (in Hourani, 1961: 35–70); and fifth 'The Ottoman Empire' (in Hourani, 1962: 25–33).

The Ottoman Background of the Modern Middle East

standing of the behaviour of the Arab states. The topic is perhaps seen as boring, not in vogue, and is also quite demanding for, as Hourani suggested, any critical treatment of this matter would require a search of Ottoman archives, not only in Cairo but also in Istanbul. This implies a fair — and probably quite rare — command of both Arabic and Turkish (see 'The Present State of Islamic and Middle Eastern Historiography', in Hourani, 1980: 167–9).

Still, Hourani sheds light on some of the most profound themes, which could serve as a basis for more than one important study of the modern Middle East. For example, in 1946 he wrote:

> Over a large part of the Arab and Islamic worlds, the spiritual and social unity which they possessed was reinforced by the political unity derived from common membership of the Ottoman Empire. The positive virtue of Ottoman rule was that it provided this political unity; it's negative that it did not interfere with the life and customary law of the subject-peoples. Nomad by origin, the Ottoman Turks cared little for the arts of peace, commerce, and industry or for culture. They left them to others, and thus contributed nothing essential to the civilization of the Arab provinces which they ruled for four hundred years. In conquering the Arab world, they themselves had been conquered by it.
> (Hourani, 1946b: 68)

And 22 years later he wrote:

> Many of the things Middle Eastern countries have in common can be explained by their having been ruled for

so long by the Ottomans; many of the things which differentiate them can be explained by the different ways in which they emerged from the Ottoman empire.

('The Ottoman Background of the Modern Middle East', in Hourani, 1981: 17)

Additional statements can be cited, but the two above are the most comprehensive, and representative of the kind of issues Hourani raised. Yet Hourani was not systematic in writing about Ottoman rule; his writings were scattered and relatively short. Thus, for our purposes here, his ideas need to be cohesively brought together. Such a careful rearrangement leads to the following: the Ottoman Empire was a 'Muslim State', but what is a Muslim State? The empire was an 'Empire of the Cities' ('The Ottoman Empire', in Hourani, 1962a: 31) — Islamic cities — but what, then, is an Islamic city? The Islamic city was dominated by the politics of 'notables'. Who are they and what function did they serve? In other words, what was the relationship between the centre (Istanbul) and the periphery (the provincial cities)?

With the exception of Morocco and parts of Arabia, from the beginning of the early part of the sixteenth century until the First World War, the Ottoman Empire dominated what we now refer to as the 'Arab World'. The Ottomans were late arrivals to the Muslim world. They filled 'the vacuum left by the collective failure of the Arab will in Abbasid days' ('Race, Religion and Nation-state,' in Hourani, 1961: 76). Coming from afar, from the tribes of Central Asia, they used as a source of legitimacy their rule of an Islamic state, a state with an absolute but just ruler, which kept the unity of the *umma* (the community of believers), defended Islam from Christian attack, and restored the rule of doctrinal orthodoxy against that of Shi'ism and Ismailism (Hourani, 1962a: 13). The Ottoman Empire passionately invoked the notion of 'social harmony', the idea of society kept in harmony and balance by a just and absolute ruler (interview with Hourani, Oxford, 14 May 1991).

For many centuries Muslims viewed the state in terms of religion and dynasty. The legitimacy of the ruler — in our case the Sultan — depended upon his enforcement of the *shari'a* (a system of morality and observed codes of Islamic law). Thus, the Ottoman Empire served the function of an 'Islamic state'. In its early days the Ottoman Empire was only one of several Turkish sultanates, but two events — the conquest of Constantinople in 1453 and the occupation of Egypt, Syria and the Hijaz between 1516 and 1917 — changed its nature. According to Hourani, the latter made the young empire the greatest Muslim power of its time and brought with it contact with the great ancient Muslim urban civilizations where Islamic theology and law flourished and where tradition was nourished in the great schools of Damascus, Aleppo and Cairo ('The Ottoman Background of the Modern Middle East', in Hourani, 1981: 6–7).

The conquest of the great Arab cities also brought Turks into contact with the urban classes that were to serve as instruments of balance between government and its underlying societies. Most important was the new control of the holy places, which added a different dimension to the empire. The Holy Cities enhanced the empire's Muslim character and reinforced legitimacy in its role as defender of Islam and the holy places.

The characteristics of the Ottoman Empire revealed the terms of its social contract. The empire defended Islam and preserved Arab civilization. It was the guarantor of the continuity of Islamic culture and tradition. Moreover, it extended the bounds of Islam north to the southern and eastern parts of Europe, and east to southern Asia. More importantly, the Ottoman state met the Hobbesian bargain — it provided stability, security and political order, protected the roads of pilgrimage and kept the trade routes secure. Its commander, and focus of all loyalty, was the Sultan, and its power base lay inside the walls of the great cities of Islam ('The Ottoman Background of the Modern Middle East', in Hourani, 1981: 3–6).

The Ottoman Empire was the custodian of Arab civilization and the Islamic cities of the Arab provinces were where this civilization and culture were kept alive. This postulation was one of the major themes (if not the major theme) of Hourani's *A History of the Arab Peoples* (1991a). But even before Hourani wrote of the 'Islamic city', its habitat and way of life, his critical analysis of the work of other scholars revealed many important observations about the nature of Arab societies under Ottoman rule (Hourani, 1970). The Islamic city existed in its traditional form from the AD seventh century until the beginning of modern times. It was Islamic in the sense that its urban structure evolved around the mosque and the markets (*suqs*) (see also Raymond, 1985: 13) and that its personality and way of life were organized by the rules of Islam:

> The congregational mosque in the centre of the city, the religious schools beneath its shadow, the hierarchy of *suqs*, whose position in relation to mosque and schools was determined by the religious role of the goods they sold or the attitude of the *shari'a* towards them, the residential quarters with their ethnic or religious solidarity, the cemeteries and shrines of saints outside

the walls; all these, they suggested, existed and were where they were because the city was a Muslim city.

(Hourani, 1970: 22)

In some sense this quotation reflects what Hourani had observed from the work of the French scholars Georges and William Marçais (Hourani, 1970). His agreement with them was followed by his disagreement with Max Weber. The German sociologist presumed that a city, in the full sense, has to be mutually and exclusively made up of five components: markets; fortifications; a court administering a relatively independent law; distinctive forms of urban association; and, finally, partial autonomy (Hourani, 1970: 23). According to Weber, the city existed in Europe but never in Asia and only for a short period and only in parts of the Near East. Hourani believed that such a presumption was an example of the European tendency to stereotype the East. If, indeed, we accept Weber's points, we will reject the existence of such phenomenon as an 'Islamic city'. The Muslim city met only two of Weber's five requirements: it never possessed autonomy, never had a political centre,[4] nor did it have its own independent law. Why, and how, should it if the *shari'a* was the only law recognized by Islam and the autonomy of the city was overshadowed by the state whose power was rooted within its walls? Also, the 'Islamic city' was never allowed to have an urban form of

---

4. André Raymond, an influential former student of Hourani, wrote (Raymond, 1985: 13): 'In the structuring of urban centres, the market and the Great Mosque played the decisive role, that of the political centre being generally limited if not nonexistent.'

association. That would run counter to the spirit of Islamic social philosophy, which was against the formation of special interest groups (economic or social) since such associations might lead to an 'exclusive natural solidarity hostile to the all-including solidarity of an *umma* based on common obedience to God's commands' (Hourani, 1970: 24).

But it is mistaken to assume that because the Islamic city did not have autonomy it was politically passive. True enough, with the lack of political centres and formal institutions, the Islamic city did not play as elaborate a role as that of its European counterparts. It had its own role to play though. According to Hourani, this role can be understood through the idea of basic harmony between the central government and the 'agro-city' (Hourani, 1970: 26). It was a two-way relationship; government needed the city surplus and the city yearned for state protection. The Islamic city never got too close to, and never strayed too far from, the source of political power. The city and its elite played mediator between the central government and the common man.

According to Hourani, the relationship between government and urban communities during the Ottoman age should be seen against the backdrop of two factors. First, political power was always in the hands of a non-Arab military of Turkish origin, 'Islamised but not always deeply so, and standing at a certain distance from the Arabic or Persian-speaking peoples whom they ruled' (Hourani, 1970: 28). Second was the strong connection between the two groups that assumed the responsibilities of urban leadership — the *'ulama*, and the commercial bourgeoisie. There were many marriages between the two groups and many members of the bourgeoisie sent their children to religious schools to become *'ulama*. More important, both groups had a common interest in order and stability. The commercial bourgeoisie demanded government protection of trade routes and sometimes even expected the government to create new ones. The *'ulama* wanted to maintain control over the *awqaf* (religious endowments), the source of their economic power and social prestige. True, the absence of formal institutions and the informal exercise of power make it very difficult to define political roles. To do so, we must look at the relationship and the close cooperation between men of the sword and men of the bazaar, what Hourani called the 'politics of notables', his creative and pioneering approach to explain what was really happening in, and to, the Arab provinces under Ottoman rule.[5] Indeed, Hourani asserted that only the study of the dynamics of change and exchange between the urban notables and the central government can give us the tools with which to analyse what was really taking place.

The old division of history in terms of states and dynasties was not without its value; the imposition, for example, of Ottoman rule on the western part of the Muslim world was an event of great importance, however we look at it. But it is too simple and therefore misleading to go beyond that and make a further distinction simply in terms of the strength or weakness of Ottoman rule; the traditional division of a period of

---

5. Equal credit must go to Ira Lapidus, a scholar at Berkeley who was simultaneously applying the same method using the 'politics of notables'. While Hourani's work covered the Ottoman age, that of Lapidus concentrated on the Mamluk period. The two scholars knew one another but were unaware at the time of each other's work (see Lapidus, 1967).

Ottoman greatness followed by one of Ottoman decline does not help us much to find out what really happened.
('Ottoman Reform and the Politics of Notables', Hourani, 1981: 36)

Hourani perceived the importance of the local leaders (urban notables) and the role they had to play in a society no longer controlled or ruled by the natives of the land. The notables understood their own society better than those outside rulers who happened to be Muslim and nothing more. In their turn the notables could convey the ideas of the ruler downward into society, and at the same time could also apply pressure on the ruler, should that ruler somehow not govern as effectively as he ought. In fact, the notables were social and cultural intermediaries. Hourani and Lapidus (see note 5 above) were each able to show in their own ways that religious and commercial leadership overlapped and that there was a much wider class, or stratum, of society than just that represented by the mosque. For Hourani, a genuine understanding of society is not achieved by isolating either its top or its bottom. Rather, it requires an understanding of how directives from top to bottom were made, how power and information get distributed in a society, the response of the society, and how that response is transmitted upwards.

Hourani's study of Ottoman history can be divided into two periods. The first stretched from 1760 to 1860 and reflected a decline of Ottoman power; the control of the central government was weakened or was increasingly exercised in an indirect way. The second period began in 1860 and ended with the fall of the empire in 1914. In this period, through the process of reforms — Tanzimat — the empire tried to regain central control and to recapture its lost power. Instead, during

The Ottoman Background of the Modern Middle East

this time the empire lost all but its Arab provinces. For practical purposes this large, once nearly universal empire became a Turco-Arab state. Hourani's ultimate reason in selecting these two periods was that they reflected many important aspects of the struggle for modernization and that throughout these years one can see the crystallization and the changes in the power of the notables.

There were two pillars to a notable's sphere of influence. First, he must have access to authority and thus an ability to mediate between the ruler and society. A notable must also have a power base of his own, whether economic, social, or religious. Such power had to originate from within and could not be dependent upon the ruler. The notables had to tread carefully. They could be neither instruments of the ruler nor enemies of authority. At times coalitions of urban and rural forces had formed, but never to a degree sufficient to consolidate power in the hands of any one part of the notables.

> In such political systems there is a tendency toward the formation of two or more coalitions roughly balancing one another, and for this several reasons may be given: leadership of this kind is *not* an institution, and there will always be those who challenge it; since the leader has to combine so many interests, and to balance them against the interests of the ruler, he is bound to disappoint some groups, who therefore tend to leave his coalition for another; and it is in the interest of the ruler to create and maintain rivalries among his powerful subjects, as otherwise he may find the whole of society drawn up against him.
> ('Ottoman Reform and the Politics of Notables', in Hourani, 1981: 41–2; my emphasis)

A logical conclusion to be drawn from all of this is that the role of the notables as social intermediaries embodied caution as well as hypocrisy. The job was never smooth, simple or easy. In Hourani's lucid description:

> In general their actions must be circumspect: the use of influence in private; the cautious expression of discontent, by absenting themselves from the ruler's presence; the discreet encouragement of opposition — but not up to the point where it may call down the fatal blow of the ruler's anger.
>
> ('Ottoman Reform and the Politics of Notables', in Hourani, 1981: 42)

Another sensitive aspect of their job was that they had to succeed in three dimensions — first on the local level, with the notables' own people; second on an 'official' level with the Ottoman agent sent from abroad; and third on the 'imperial' level, since the centre of all political power was Istanbul.

Istanbul had its own mystique. Beneath the city existed the culture of old Byzantium. Its trade lay in the hands of foreigners and members of religious minorities. Unlike the traditional Muslim cities under its rule, Istanbul had no ancient Islamic society. Thus, according to Hourani, its politics were not the politics of notables, but rather the politics of the court or the bureaucracy ('Ottoman Reform and the Politics of Notables', in Hourani, 1981: 43).

Although political relations between Istanbul and its Arab provincial centres were dominated by the politics of the notables as intermediaries, such politics differed from place to place. Not surprisingly, the Ottoman control was generally less direct in areas relatively distant from the capital of the empire, and tighter in areas closer to the centre of power. In Cairo the balance was more even; Egypt was viewed as too important to be ruled loosely for too long ('Ottoman Reform and the Politics of Notables', in Hourani, 1981: 45–6). Therefore, from time to time, the Ottomans asserted their authority to keep up the prestige of the Sultan as the defender of Islam and the holy places. On the other hand, in Acre and Baghdad the Ottomans accepted the Mamluk monopoly of power. Both were frontier posts — Baghdad located on the southern frontier of Persia with its majority of potentially disloyal Shi'is, and Acre being too close to an almost independent Egypt and open to the hill country of southern Lebanon and northern Palestine, areas which in the past had shown great tendencies towards independence and a willingness to ally themselves with foreign powers. Hence, it was in the interest of the Porte to allow rein to such groups as could provide sufficient armed forces, collect taxes, and yet remain loyal to the Sultan as overlord ('Ottoman Reform and the Politics of Notables', in Hourani, 1981: 47). Mosul was similar in that local groups there were able to maintain their own ruler, but here the governor came from a local family that had no relation to a Mamluk household ('Ottoman Reform and the Politics of Notables', in Hourani, 1981: 48).

But, as Hourani saw it, the story was quite different in the cities of Syria and the Hijaz: here Ottoman control was more tangible. Here were the Holy Cities of Islam, and the pilgrim routes that had to be controlled by no one but the Sultan. Here were to be found the 'politics of notables' in their purest form. Unlike in other regions, here the notables were not of a Mamluk group but were from ancient families of bourgeoisie and 'ulama. Some of these notables were members of the governor's court, or *divan*, which gave them continuous and direct access to him. In fact, at times the notables made it difficult for the ruler to rule without them for they had their own power base and independent sources of wealth from land and trade routes to the Holy Cities and across the desert to Baghdad, Persia and the Gulf.

Throughout the seventeenth to the nineteenth centuries the notables — be they Syrian or from Cairo or Baghdad and whether their relationship to Istanbul was tangible or not — all had one role to play: to facilitate the process of governing between the Ottoman Empire and its Arab provinces. But the environment in which they operated was changing and to that they had to adjust: the Ottoman Empire was entering the 'age of decline'.

By the beginning of the nineteenth century the empire was experiencing symptoms of internal as well as external weakness. Hourani emphasizes that the disintegration of the Sultan's power was the source of internal decay. Indeed, there were attempts to shift the centre of power from Sultan to Grand Vizier. But the role of Grand Vizier was no substitute for that of Sultan. After all, the position itself did not carry the same prestige as Sultan. Nor was the Grand Vizier certain of his tenure in office. But as the central authority of the empire was shrinking, communal authority became much stronger (Hourani, 1961: 39).

Something greater was amiss. The source of imperial strength, the balance that for over two hundred years had regulated its societies, was no longer there. The decline of central power in the Islamic state meant the imperial government could no longer give 'a defence against disorder and a system of law regulating the relationship of man and man' ('Fertile Crescent in The Eighteenth Century', in Hourani, 1961: 41). Thus, Hourani saw that the Ottoman dilemma had, in large part, a moral dimension; the decay of Ottoman power was not just physical (or military). For example, in more than one place, Hourani hints that all the Ottomans wanted from Europe was Western technology pure and simple. The Ottomans failed to realize that technology must not merely be learned (for examples see Hourani, 1962a: 42, 53) and that success required not only the borrowing of technology but also an importing of the spirit of enlightenment, which led to technological developments.

Externally, the empire was facing economic and political upheaval. The rapid European geographical expansion was leading to the establishment of European trading centres in the Indian Ocean, which, in turn, had a negative effect on the pattern of trade between the empire and the rest of the world. In addition, the discovery of America led to a flow of silver and gold into the Mediterranean countries and a high rate of inflation in the empire. This inflation disturbed the system of finance within the Ottoman Empire and brought hardship to the productive classes. The final outcome of this economic crisis was the depopulation of the countryside, the decline of agriculture and — in some cases — the disappearance of some of the traditional crafts (Hourani, 1962a: 41).

Politically the empire also faced tremendous pressure from Europe. The Ottomans had learned from the West in the past: in the sixteenth century, for example, they put to good use gunpowder, new navigation techniques and naval strategy. But increasingly they could not keep up with the achievements of the Western scientific revolution. As Hourani puts it, 'the scientific discoveries aroused no echo.' This became all too obvious by the middle of the eighteenth century when the evidence of decline was too strong to be ignored (Hourani, 1962a: 41). The empire was no longer capable of defending itself from the expanding European influence and was losing its grip on most of its regions. The Ottomans had to find European allies against their European adversaries. Such manoeuvring led to the large-scale opening of the empire to the ways of the West and its new military techniques. This consequently led to the formation of the first group of political westernizers in the Middle East. In such a climate, and under such circumstances, the empire was faced with the problem of how to maintain its Islamic persona yet introduce change, create institutions and a political morality, all of which, in the modern world, were keys to strength. In short, the Ottoman state had to rethink its position. It had no option but to reform.

In the period between 1839 and 1878 the Porte adopted the idea of the Tanzimat, or reforms. Supposedly, the objective of the reforms was to institute a uniform and centralized administrative system that would enable the central government to work directly with each citizen according to rational principles of justice and equality. On the issue of the Tanzimat, we find Hourani and the prominent historian of modern Turkey, Bernard Lewis, in full agreement. Lewis saw the rationale behind the Tanzimat as less will to reform than manoeuvring for political, rather than social or legal, reform (Lewis, 1961: 167). Hourani described them as 'piecemeal reforms' (Hourani, 1962a: 45). This was because they did not touch the heart of the Ottoman problem of legal and moral reform. Rather, they produced an arbitrary and absolutist government with, on the one hand a Sultan who sought absolute power and, on the other, a bureaucracy that now expected power to be restrained by regulations and principles. Still, as Hourani reminds us, we should not underestimate the reforms ('The Ottoman Background of the Modern Middle East', in Hourani, 1981: 14). The method of administration and justice did change. The Ottomans gained back their lost central control and were able to improve the amenities of life and to make some improvements in the infrastructure of larger cities and seaports. Moreover, there were many improvements in the positions of non-Muslim minorities.

Aside from these political changes, the reforms brought important changes in the social order, changes whose impact continued beyond the empire's existence. First, on the economic side, as the Middle East became more and more attached to the European trading system as a 'plantation economy' ('The Ottoman Background of the Modern Middle East', in Hourani, 1981: 15), it became a net producer of raw materials and an almost absolute importer of manufactured goods. Second, the Tanzimat were responsible for changes on the intellectual side of things;

> There was an intellectual change, produced by new schools, the coming of the printing press and newspapers, the translation of books from English or French, travel, and the experience of living in a world dominated by Europe. Among officials, officers, teachers and merchants, there spread new ideas about how society should be organised: in particular, the idea that it should be organised on a basis of nationalism, of a sentiment of national loyalty and unity in which members of different religious or social communities should join; a nationalism explicitly secular but having, like everything in the Middle East, a concealed religious element, it was because of this perhaps that the idea of an 'Ottoman' nation proved too fragile to resist more limited and robust national ideas; first Serbs and Greeks, then

Romanians and Bulgarians created their own nation-states, then the idea spread to the Armenians, then to the Turks themselves, and to other Muslim peoples, Arabs, Albanians and Kurds.

('The Ottoman Background of the Modern Middle East', in Hourani, 1981: 16)

Third, and based on the above, there came the expansion of Europe which played a major role in the direction of reforms ('The Ottoman Background of the Modern Middle East', in Hourani, 1981: 16). European help to the reformers was given as long as it did not harm Western interests such as the passage to India and the direct and free access to the subjects of the empire ('Ottoman Reform and the Politics of Notables', in Hourani, 1981: 64). Hourani points out that, beginning in the seventeenth century the interests of European states in the Near East were becoming more determined. Each state had its own interests to preserve and further, interests secured and maintained by the different embassies and consulates, especially those of France, Britain and Russia. By the nineteenth century, with the explosion in trade, European governments were no longer satisfied with the old ways. Unwilling to continue to seek the cooperation of whatever government office might be of help, and instead of working through the existing Ottoman framework, they began to select their own. Their embassies and consulates became increasingly influential and, through them, the different European powers established direct contact with various groups, especially Christian and Jewish merchants who, for reasons of their own, wanted European protection and were therefore willing to collaborate.

Overwhelmed by the power of Europe, an increasingly

enfeebled Ottoman state had no choice but to cooperate. Europeans needed a certain kind of Ottoman government, one in which they enjoyed a special place in the sun. On the other hand, the Ottoman Empire needed the armies of one European power to protect it against the threats of another ('Ottoman Reform and the Politics of Notables', in Hourani, 1981: 63).

Even so, the status quo was not maintained; one by one the Arab provinces were entering the 'age of colonialism', the age of direct European rule. In 1830 Algeria was lost to French rule, Tunisia in 1881. Egypt fell under British control in 1882, and by 1912 Libya was in Italian hands. Even those parts of the Arab world that remained to the end under Ottoman control were subject to increasing European social and economic influence. For example, in the still Ottoman-ruled Fertile Crescent, European powers had direct access to both government and the local populace and therefore began to play the part of intermediaries, a role that had belonged for so long to the urban notables. Thus, the reforms and their aftermath were a turning point in the history of the Empire and its Arab regions.

Full credit must go to Hourani as the first to show the assorted reactions of the different Arab provinces to the reforms and to explain the reasons why some notables cooperated and some did not (Sadowski n.d.: 17–21).[6] But before moving to examine what was taking place in Cairo or in the Fertile Crescent, we must look to the imperial capital of Istanbul. Unlike the politics of notables in the Arab provinces, the politics in Istanbul had always been that of the court or the bureaucracy. Those who were in charge of implementing the

---

6. Unpublished essay. Sadowski gave the author a copy and permission to use it.

reforms had to interact with several old and deeply rooted institutions. But the reforms were able to break the Janissary regiments, and to weaken palace influence. The institution that was the main benefactor of reform was the higher bureaucracy whose military rivals had been eliminated and who saw more demand for their services as the only group qualified to run the administrative system. Most of these came from families with a long tradition in public service. Hourani described them as a solid group of men who had common values and ideas about which direction the empire should take; they had certain beliefs about Europe, its civilization and its system of justice, efficiency, and rationality ('Ottoman Reform and the Politics of Notables', in Hourani, 1981: 55). Above all, the higher bureaucracy believed that its own existence and that of the empire were entwined, and that shoring up the strength of the empire was therefore essential. But the bureaucracy was not uncontested. The palace had its own vision and way of doing things, although its power and wealth were weakened. The Sultan still remained the focal point of loyalty, and Sultan Abdülhamid II was to break the division of power between the bureaucracy and the palace ('Ottoman Reform and the Politics of Notables', in Hourani, 1981: 57).

Furthermore, the government was getting weaker as a result of ever-increasing European influences, which even touched upon the internal affairs of the empire. Higher Ottoman officials became identified with different European embassies. Also, there was what Hourani called the 'new instruments of action' ('Ottoman Reform and the Politics of Notables', in Hourani, 1981: 56), which included the activities of the intelligentsia and its use of the press. The Young Ottomans, a group of Turkish intellectuals, believed in the ideas of Enlightenment and gave the reforms their most formidable critique.

The work of Serif Mardin — for which Hourani had great respect — shows us that this was the first group in Ottoman history to organize political protest and to utilize the new instrument of political action (Mardin, 1962: 4).

In Cairo, change came in a less complicated fashion. There, Muhammad Ali, whose first objective was simply to destroy all rivals to his power, carried out the reforms independently of Istanbul. He was successful where his predecessors had failed, and created around himself a strong 'Mamluk' household that knew of none but him, and had loyalty to none but him. He well realized that military science and technology was needed and could only be acquired from Europe, the source as well of less desirable concepts. Hourani described Muhammad Ali's trepidations in his writings on the nature of the Arab dilemma in modern history:

> He [Muhammad Ali] needed artillery officers, doctors, and engineers. It was not his intention that they should acquire more than a necessary skill: they were kept under strict control, and when a group of students asked his permission to make a tour of France and acquire a knowledge of French life he refused it. But with the new skills new ideas were bound to enter, and the schools and scholastic missions had an influence greater far than he could have intended.
> (Hourani, 1962a: 53)

Like the rulers in Istanbul, Muhammad Ali was willing to carry through reform as long as it did not affect his monopoly. He adopted whatever principles or ideas he thought could work to enhance his own power and omitted — or rather ignored — those he perceived would threaten his position.

Thus it is obvious that the reforms in Egypt (however implemented) worked in the interest of the ruler and against those of the notables. The chief loser there was the old merchant class. It lost much of its wealth and power as a result of the opening of the Red Sea to steam navigation and the growth of large-scale cotton trade with Europe, since that trade was controlled by European or local Christian or Jewish merchants. Muhammad Ali's absolutism and the absence of any other instruments of political action or expression were virtually responsible for the disappearance of the 'politics of notables'.

By the late 1870s all this had changed. Men who lacked Muhammad Ali's strength and leadership ruled Egypt. The power of the ruler was decreasing as the pressure of foreign powers increased ('Ottoman Reform and the Politics of Notables', in Hourani, 1981: 53). Once more the door was opened for the return of the politics of notables, and it found its niche under the indirect rule of British occupation. It was a brief triumph; by the end of the 1890s, the British began to change their style and, with direct rule, once again put an end to the politics of notables.

The story of the reforms in the cities of the Fertile Crescent differs from that of Istanbul, or even Cairo. The ideas of Europe were late arrivals for the Arab Muslims here, who did not experience, as did their counterparts in Egypt, the social and intellectual trauma of European occupation. Unlike the Egyptians, Syrian notables — until the end — did not play an active role in imperial administration. Rather, their role was limited to 'local politics' (Hourani, 1962a: 54). According to Hourani, Christian minorities in the Fertile Crescent were exposed to European ideas long before everyone else. Even so there was not much they could do, for they lived in a state that was actively reasserting its Islamic identity (Hourani, 1962a: 67). It was not until the end of the last century that the great Muslim families of Syria ceased sending their children to the traditional religious schools, instead preparing them, for the first time, for civil service positions via the professional schools. If the reforms in Istanbul and Cairo worked in the interest of the ruler against that of the subject, in the Fertile Crescent the outcome was different: aside from the competition posed by European consulates beginning in the nineteenth century, the influence of the urban notables was untouched. Indeed, it was stronger than before.

The reforms brought in their train novel policies and regulations that needed implementation: new legal codes; methods of tax collection; administrative changes. This meant there was a greater demand for the notables as social intermediaries. It was no surprise that the notables supported centralization and modernization and identified themselves with the reforms (see Hourani, 1991a: 277; for more precise information see Khoury, 1983: 53). Yet, as Hourani points out, we must not assume that the notables were willing to allow the reforms to be carried out to their final conclusion of centralization — namely, the establishment of a direct relationship between the subject and the central government, eliminating their function as intermediaries. Moreover, the 'ulama felt that reforms would pull the rug out from under their feet. The doctrines of the Western enlightenment and of modernization were alien and were interpreted by them as the work of 'innovators' going against the rules of Islam. Besides the 'ulama were the merchants, whose economic power was challenged by European consulates and foreign merchants. Due to the European influence, trading systems were no longer the same and economic centres were shifting from the old, traditional cities of the interior to the coastal towns. The expansion of European trade and influence gave more economic power to Christian and Jewish merchants who were well-connected with the various consulates. Even the notables' hold on the land was challenged; in large parts of Syria, Christian and Jewish merchants replaced the traditional landowners as the financiers and organizers of agricultural production. Thus, the honeymoon that the notables had enjoyed in the wake of the reforms was short-lived. Indeed, by the 1860s, just about twenty years after their adoption by the Ottoman government, the reforms were to be strongly opposed by the notables.

Hourani does not make clear the connection between Ottomanism and Arabism. He also fails to provide us with a complete analysis of the process that went into the transformation from Ottomanism to Arabism. However, it was Hourani who told us that it is to this process that we need to look for a better understanding of how Arab states — with all their differences and similarities — emerged from the ruins of Ottomanism. To some degree, statements throughout his work allude to this transformation as the result of many factors:

- the failure of the empire to fulfill the terms of its social contract as the defender of the nation of Islam;
- the infringement of Europe;
- the emulation of European-style nationalism by provinces of the empire; and finally
- the growth of a strict Turkish nationalism.

(Hourani, 1991a: 308–10)[7]

---

7. See also 'The Ottoman Background of the Modern Middle East', in Hourani, 1981: 18.

Hourani's main emphasis in this subject is to focus on the role of the Syrian notables, correctly enough since, after all, Arabism was primarily Syrian in origin. As we have seen, the reforms were never carried to their logical conclusion and thus did not break the power of the notables who instead took from them whatever they thought would strengthen their position. In addition, the 'Hamidian policy', named after Sultan Abdülhamid, helped to maintain their position. By the end of the nineteenth century, the empire had lost all its European provinces and had been reduced to a Turco-Arab state. The Sultan began to emphasize the Islamic persona of the empire. In doing so, he 'pampered' (Khoury, 1983: 54) Arab notables in Damascus and other Syrian towns. The notables of Syria started sending their children to Istanbul to be trained and prepared for work in the imperial civil or military services. Considering the privileged position of these notables, what then was it, what took place, that pushed the elites to abandon Ottomanism and adopt the idea of Arabism, later to crystallize into Arab nationalism?

It is rather naive to search for a short answer to such a question. The work of both Philip Khoury and C. Ernest Dawn suggests that several elements contributed to the transformation from Ottomanism to Arabism. Two points need to be kept in mind. The first is that Arabism in its early stages (from the end of the nineteenth century until 1908) (Dawn, 1973: 149) was an 'apolitical' movement, mainly a cultural movement advocating love of the homeland (*watan*) and the revival of the Arabic language and heritage. Love for the homeland was natural and well-established among Muslims, though it had never before been articulated with a political significance. Muslims never considered nationality to be connected with territoriality (Dawn, 1973: 13).

In fact, Hourani was quite right to suggest that George Antonius was inaccurate when he assumed that Arab territorial-nationalism had emerged much earlier ('The Arab Awakening Forty Years Later', in Hourani, 1981: 202–3; for Antonius's view, see Hourani, 1981: 36–60). Hardly any Ottoman Arab questioned the right of the Turks to rule. After all, the Ottoman Empire was the nation of Islam with the Sultan as its just guardian. Second, Arabism and Ottomanism had the same origin; both ideologies were initiated as responses to Western hegemony, both were concerned with the defence of Islam and denying that Western culture was superior to that of the East.

According to Dawn, until 1914 the aims of Arabism did not differ much from those of Ottomanism, but as the latter failed to close the gap between Islam and the West, many Ottomanists crossed over to Arabism (Dawn, 1973: 124). Khoury went one step farther when he showed that Ottomanism took a different turn as the Young Turks (who came to power in 1908) began adopting the politics of Turcification.[8] The imposition of Turkish language and national identity presented something that the 'ulama of Damascus and its notables totally rejected ('Damascus Notables and the Rise of Arab Nationalism before World War I', in Khoury, 1983: 58). Hourani added that in this new wave of Turkish nationalism, ideas of a 'Turkish people' were developed by Turkish intellectuals who presumed all Muslims of the empire to be 'potential Turks and, once they

---

8. For the impact of the Young Turks on the Arab provinces, see 'The Impact of the Young Turk Revolution in the Arab Speaking Provinces of the Ottoman Empire', in Kedourie, 1974: 124–61.

had the power, ... tried to Turkize all Moslems by force' ('Race, Religion and Nation-State', in Hourani, 1961: 83–4). Such behaviour aroused a defensive nationalism among those Arabs and others (Albanians and Kurds) who were loyal to the Sultan, yet did not wish to accept the imposition of a Turkish identity. The Albanians — who had always been pillars of the empire — revolted and proclaimed their independence in 1912. And the loyal Kurds — who had played a large role in defending the frontier against Persia — began to organize their own national groups for independence. Finally, in 1916, there was the Arab revolt and its aftermath. Soon after, the imperial Ottoman order, which had lasted for centuries, came crashing down.

For the Arabs this was a bewildering moment; the former subjects of a great empire were faced with the questions 'Who am I?' and 'What am I now?' (interview with Hourani, Oxford, 19 May 1991). The old cities of the Arab world were no longer protected and suddenly found themselves naked before the European might. Face to face with the outside world, they had little going for them — a nationalism that was vague in its goals and a knowledge that was limited in its understanding of the harsh realities of statecraft. As Hourani suggested, the new situation in which the Arabs found themselves was difficult and sad. Most Arabs who joined the rebellion later regretted having done so — the Ottoman legacy still retained a power all its own:

> At the meetings which founded the Arab League in 1944–45, many observers must have been struck by the Ottoman as well as the Arab links between those who spoke for the various Arab states east of Egypt: they had been at school together in Istanbul; they had a common

way of looking at the world; behind the vision of Arab unity lay memories of a lost imperial grandeur.
> ('Ottoman Background of the Modern Middle East', in Hourani, 1981: 18)

Hourani's work on the Ottoman age opens a large world. His analysis gives a profound description of the relationship that existed between Istanbul and its Arab provinces, and he is able to show that relations were kept to a minimum. The social contract was Hobbesian in its nature — protection and order in exchange for money and loyalty. For the most part, and at most times, the great Arab cities were left alone to handle their affairs. Throughout history these cities had not been interested in political power *per se*. They were merchant cities; the bazaar was paramount. These cities were 'politically practical' and had no problem living with a new power broker from outside their walls. Should that broker lose ground, they would not hesitate to bid him farewell and welcome the next Sultan. Also, Hourani shows us the importance of 'class analysis' and its applicability to the study of the Arab Middle East. His analysis of the urban notables and their role as social middlemen between the subject and the central government gives us a solid framework of sociological analysis. Yet, because his analysis speaks little about the subject, there is a tendency to overestimate the role, and the activities, of the urban notables.

Nevertheless, a few points — some of great relevance — are lacking in his work. In his assessment of the decline of the Ottoman Empire, he assigns too much weight to the position and the role of the Sultan. He uses — and sometimes overuses — Ibn Khaldun's theory of rise and decline. He is most successful in applying the ascent part but fails (or refuses to deal with) its descent. Hourani does not make the connection between the empire's last military expansion and the beginning of its decline, nor does he ask if it is mere coincidence that the two events took place at the same time. Although the work of Raymond was dear to him, he does not pay close attention to it, nor does he investigate the earlier suggestion that Arab cities did not have to carry the burden of protection against the threat from former powers. Raymond wrote that:

> The larger Arab cities show, moreover, in their very structure, traces of this long standing inclusion in an empire that was vast, powerful, and relatively well protected from outside aggression.
> ('The Ottoman Empire and Arab Cities', in Raymond, 1985: 2)

Hence, a central question was neglected: what happens and what are the effects on the progress of a particular civilization when society — in the military and political sense — is not required to worry about threat from outside?

It also seems that Hourani's judgement of the Ottoman Empire changed over time. In his earlier writings he held a harsh view. He saw the Ottoman as an uncultured, militant intruder who had no contribution to make to Arab civilization (Hourani, 1946b: 68). His later writings show a kinder, more sympathetic view. In these later contributions he came to write of the Ottomans as the defenders of Islam, the power that helped keep continuity of Arab culture and civilization.[9]

---

9. This was one of his main themes when he wrote of the Ottoman age in *A History of the Arab Peoples* (1991a: 207–81).

Regardless, his analysis of the subject leaves us no doubt that the Ottoman age must not be neglected. According to Hourani, 'the greatest task of the present generation of Middle Eastern historians is perhaps to explore this Ottoman world' (Hourani, 1991c: 129). In other words, the Ottoman imperial past must be recovered if the new world of the 'successor states' and of nationalism is to be really understood.

3

The Intellectual Origins of Arab Nationalism

There are striking similarities between the life experiences of Albert Hourani and those of the great chronicler of Arab nationalism, George Antonius. The scholar Donald Reid wrote:

> Like Antonius, Hourani came of Lebanese Christian stock, advised the British on their Middle Eastern policies, and felt an urgent mission to bridge the gap between Britain and the Arabs. Neither Antonius nor Hourani regarded these efforts as particularly successful. Hourani retired into detached scholarship; death overtook Antonius early, and we do not know the path he might have chosen.
>
> (Reid, 1982: 553–4)

Had Antonius not died prematurely in 1942, he would have shared disappointment with Hourani, beginning with the loss of Palestine in 1948, and ending with the tragic events of the 1990 Iraqi invasion of Kuwait.

Arab nationalism would, in time, disappoint the liberal intellectuals who fastened on it their extravagant hopes. Men like Antonius and Hourani, intellectuals who believed in the primacy of ideas, who assumed that a world of Arab nations would be a liberal world, were fated to experience great disillusionment with the course that Arab nationalism would take in the age of mass politics.

For Hourani, the romance of Arab nationalism and his commitment to it began quite early in his career. It was a natural concern, given his interest in political ideas. He would stay with this pursuit from the time he was introduced to it at the American University of Beirut until the very end.[1] He began with enthusiasm but was to change into a cautious observer of the phenomenon as mass-based politics remade Arab nationalism and changed it into a popular political movement.

Hourani remembered the early intellectual environment in which he had picked up the 'givens' of Arab nationalism. He took it for granted that without the impediments of British and French rule and the artificial boundaries imposed after the First World War, a united Arab nation would emerge (Hourani, 1991e: 32–3).

A man given to ideas and the written text, Hourani read the contemporary literature of Arab nationalism. T. E. Lawrence's *Seven Pillars of Wisdom* and George Antonius's *The Arab Awakening* influenced him particularly. The stylist in him would account for the great admiration he had for Lawrence. For the gifted Lawrence, the Arab world was the desert; for Hourani it was the world of the city with its notables, its

---

1. For an early example of his political view and advocacy of Arab nationalism, see his *Syria and Lebanon: A Political Essay* (Hourani, 1946b: 268–78), where he made a case for the readiness of Syria and Lebanon for independence as well as for the benefits of their subsequent unification with Iraq.

commerce and its religious life. Lawrence had gone to the Arab world unencumbered by any personal connection and had written of his freedom from the burden of any 'likeness' to the Arabs in words Hourani quoted: 'Lawrence wrote of "my solitary unlikeness, which made me no companion but an acquaintance, complete, angular, uncomfortable"' ('T. E. Lawrence and Louis Massignon', in Hourani, 1991b: 118). Hourani, the son of Lebanese immigrants, could not have this relationship to the Arab world. What drew him to Lawrence's writings were the romance and the beauty of Lawrence's language, 'so full of vivid and violent images recording the impact of a landscape, a town or a person' (Hourani, 1991b: 118).

Hourani's relationship to Antonius was more direct. As the scholar Donald Reid has indicated, there was much in the life of Antonius that was similar to Hourani's own. Antonius (1891–1942), the great publicist, had laid out the case for Arab nationalism in his powerful book *The Arab Awakening*. Though Antonius had dedicated his energies to open advocacy and Hourani chose, after some years in public life, the cloistered world of scholarship, their work and their life experiences justify the widespread sense that Hourani's work picked up where Antonius had left off. The world of Antonius was a world that Hourani knew intimately. Antonius was born to a Greek Orthodox family in the town of Dayr al-Qamar in the Shuf mountains of Lebanon. Dayr al-Qamar was not unlike Hourani's ancestral town in the south of Lebanon. When Antonius was 11 years old his family — merchants of modest means — moved to the city of Alexandria. There, Antonius attended the British-run Victoria College. Then came migration to England to study mechanical engineering, and a long period of service in the British colonial administration, which lasted

16 years and included the years of the First World War and the postwar diplomatic settlements. Antonius, very much like Hourani in the years to come, would be drawn into the struggle for Palestine and would end up disillusioned with the British Empire.

From Antonius, and from ideas popular among the politically conscious Arab intellectuals in the late 1920s and the 1930s, Hourani adopted the axiom that the new frontiers in the Arab world, imposed upon the Arab states by Britain and France, were artificial. 'Between them there are almost no natural frontiers based on either clear geographical distinction or long historical tradition' (Hourani, 1956: 130). In one of his famous essays, 'The Decline of the West in the Middle East' (1953b), he made a case to the British government for the urgency of Arab unity. He argued that a united Arab nation was unavoidable. Cultural and traditional ties too strong to be ignored had contributed to the formation of a natural community, which eventually would express itself in a 'unified political will'. The imposed frontiers — artificial or not — and the ensuing separate political authorities, would undermine the economic synergies of the Arabs. Economic, social and political stability in the Arab world could only be achieved through pan-Arabism.

Why, in Hourani's view, shouldn't the Arab nations reunite? Hourani saw quarrels between fractious Arab states as an Arab 'family' matter. It was only the competing interests of the Great Powers (and those of local politicians, dynasties and military groups) that stood as the main obstacles to Arab unity (Hourani, 1953b: 177–9). Three years later, in 1956, Hourani took a liberal, but more realistic view of the obstacles facing such unity:

Whatever the causes, the crisis of the Arab mind today is clear. All around is a sea of nihilism: the cynicism of men cut off from their own past, deprived too long of responsibility for their own fate, tied too long to a decaying Empire, exposed too soon to the corruption of wealth and power. Within the sea are four or five rocks which seem to offer the safety of a sure belief: secular nationalism, secular social democracy, liberal Islam, fundamentalist Islam, communism.

(Hourani, 1956: 131)

Although he listed many options, for him the choice was clear: secular (liberal) nationalism, or to be more specific, a liberal secularism in the style of nineteenth-century France and England. This view, first introduced by Christian Arabs of the liberal school, was always present in his heart. He believed in the welfare of the society, the freedom of individuals and, above all, the duty of the state to protect this freedom.

There was also room in Hourani's vision for 'Islamic modernism' as a supportive source of inspiration. For Hourani, 'Islamic Modernism' was

Islamic because it stood for a reassertion of the unique and perfect truth of Islam, but reformist in that it aimed at reviving what it conceived to be certain neglected elements in the Islamic tradition. But this liberal revival took place under the stimulus of European thought, and led to a gradual reinterpretation of Islamic concepts so as to make them equivalent to the guiding principles of European thought of the time. ... The effect of this, in what we called the secularizing wing of 'Abduh's school, was to bring about a *de facto* separation of the sphere of civilization from that of religion and so open another door to secular nationalism.

(Hourani, 1962a: 344)

Conflict and contradiction have their own force and should not be dismissed. A statement like the above not only reflects Hourani's idealism, but invites many questions. It is apparent here that Hourani was faced with more than one dilemma. He would like to believe, and he would like his readers to believe, that Islam and secular nationalism were compatible, that no real tension existed between the two creeds, that Arab society was ready for their enlightened coexistence, and was already on its way to an 'age of reason'. He wrote:

In the Middle East as elsewhere, men's minds have moved not only from the idea that the principles of social action are religious to the idea that they are rational, but also from the idea that there *are* such principles, standing above society, to the idea that society is its own judge and master, that the principles by which it should live are generated within itself and change as it changes, and that its own interest is the supreme principle.

('Middle Eastern Nationalism Yesterday and Today', in Hourani, 1981: 179)

Though Hourani's forecasts may not have withstood the test of time, such statements will enable us to draw a precise picture of Hourani's own conceptualization of the intellectual origins of Arab nationalism. Overall, his work insists that Arab nationalism was the product of reactions by two different groups, each with its own agenda.

The first group, and to Hourani the more important, was the Christian Arabs of the Fertile Crescent. They were the first to bring the liberal ideas of Europe to Arab lands. The second group was the moderate Islamic reformers, inspired by the example and the work of the great Muslim modernist, the Persian-born Jamal al-Din al-Afghani (1839–97) and his Egyptian associate and disciple Muhammad 'Abduh (1849–1905).

It was the two tributary streams of thought represented by these groups that had come together to form Arab nationalism. It is no exaggeration to maintain that much of Hourani's work was dedicated to following the ideas of the Christian Arabs and the inheritance of Muslim modernism. Both had their origins in a common source: the collapse of the Ottoman Empire, the erosion of an Islamic universal state. Both Christian Arabs and Muslim modernists had to find an answer to a common dilemma: the end of an imperial state had orphaned them both. For all its limitation and troubles, the Ottoman Empire had been home for over four centuries. The Ottoman tradition had anchored the lives of Muslims and Christian subjects alike, supplied them with a moral and political universe, sheltered them from the power of Europe.

This crisis of basic intellectual and moral orientation was probably severe for the Muslim Arabs. At stake was the issue for Muslims of the time: 'how to become part of the modern world while remaining Muslims?' (Hourani, 1962a: 95). Arab Christians, who were in no better position, had to answer no less agonizing a question: how to become part of the predominantly Western modern world while remaining a true Arab. Hourani never directly addressed this issue. With some sense of ambivalence he once wrote:

> Many of the Christians of Lebanon and Syria were Arab by origin, and of those who were not most had accepted the Arabic language and with it a whole culture; in a sense it was theirs but in a sense it was not, since it was an Islamic as well as an Arabic culture. These changes posed two questions for Arabic-speaking Christians: first, how to break out of their closed religious communities, which had been for so many centuries their world? ... The second question was linked with this: having broken away from the closed world of the minority, what community could they belong to?
>
> (Hourani, 1962a: 96)

The Christian Arabs hoped that liberal nationalism would provide answers to questions of that type.

Under the Ottoman Empire, Christian and Jewish minorities long lived in their closed communities, in what was known as the *millet* system. This system made it possible for these groups to maintain their social position and communal life, though it denied them entry into the military and, of course, religious organization of the empire (Hourani, 1947: 20–1). One could infer from Hourani's observations that the minorities' detachment from such obligation had helped to release their energies instead toward financial endeavours. Although the minorities clearly suffered legal disabilities relative to the empire's Muslim majority, the fact remained that all Ottoman subjects felt some sense of equality as they stood before the Sultan, who towered above all sectarian differences and stood as the focus of all loyalty (see 'Race, Religion and Nation-State in the Near East', in Hourani, 1961: 74–5). As Hourani saw it, the Ottoman Empire was a 'supra-national state' (Hourani, 1947: 119–20), large enough to be tolerant, and large enough that each nation, or *millet*, would maintain its own autonomy and culture. In spite of that, nationalism would have no effect on the political life of the state. What was it, then, that disrupted the imperial order and allowed the emergence of national identities and the end of the convenient social arrangements that had held for hundreds of years?

According to Hourani, the growing weakness of the Ottoman Empire was the main catalyst for the change in position of minorities (Hourani, 1947: 119). Still, other interrelated developments must be considered. Beginning at the end of the seventeenth century and lasting more or less until the end of the empire, the status of minorities had changed, as had the empire itself. Hourani identified two themes at play. First, the *millets* evolved into intact national groupings. The barriers between the different communities grew higher and became less flexible; in some respects what had once been religious groups became national ones ('Race, Religion and Nation-State in the Near East', in Hourani, 1961: 75). This was accelerated by the other and more important source of change: the intervention of the West and its aftermath. This was an overwhelming intervention — economic, cultural, and military — which, though it had started as early as the seventeenth century, began to exert a more tangible impact on the position of minorities as the Ottoman world moved into the nineteenth century. As Hourani had always maintained, relations between the Porte and its Christian subjects were one of the main pretexts for Western intervention. A number of European powers pressed their claim to have a special role as protectors of the Sultan's Christian subjects (Hourani, 1947: 23). Russia stepped forth as protector of the Orthodox churches, France claimed the Latin churches and Britain worked with the Protestant orders. Religion was always a cover, or convenient pretext. One capitulation by the Ottomans to one European power had to be extended to all the others. The appetite of the local Christians grew progressively. From a disadvantaged position they would ride the coattails of the Western powers to new levels of influence.

As the activities of the European powers, especially France and Great Britain, enhanced the social and economic position of minorities, growing economic connection between Europe and America brought wealth and benefit to the Levantine Christians who so often served as middlemen. Also, Westerners in the Middle East tended to hire a disproportionately large number of minorities to work in their consulates or places of business. All contributed to the rise of a new class of Levantine bourgeoisie in the large towns. It also led to the movement of large numbers of Christians from the hinterland to the cities (Hourani, 1991a: 292–8). In short, what were once closed communities became open to the outside.

If a specific date, or event, marks the new power of the West in Ottoman lands and the great intrusion of the Europeans into the affairs of the Ottoman Christians, that turning point would be the outbreak of the Crimean War in 1853. Russia had been pushing at the enfeebled Ottoman Empire. In a local religious clash between the Orthodox church and the Latin churches over control of the Church of the Holy Sepulchre in Jerusalem and the Church of the Holy Nativity in Bethlehem, the Russians had found a convenient excuse to launch war against Turkey. Russia had the upper hand, but the war was decided by British and French intervention on Turkey's side. The Ottoman Empire had escaped defeat thanks to the European balance of power. The 'sick man of Europe' was given a reprieve. But the Turks were to pay a price: the gates to the empire were to be opened to European commerce, diplomacy and intervention as never before. The Porte lost control over the city of Jerusalem, which instead became a playing field for the European consulates and the Christian world of Mount Lebanon evolved into a European protectorate.

The local Christians were more and more emboldened by the new authority of the Europeans. For the Muslims the change was like a cultural earthquake; age-old habits and ways were being undermined. The great disturbances that erupted in major urban areas in the 1850s (Aleppo in 1850, Mosul in 1854, Nablus in 1856, Jidda in 1858, Damascus in 1860), disturbances about which Hourani wrote with frequency, were the anguished response of the Muslim merchants and notables to the new dislocations. The foreign consulates now vied with local leaders for power and influence. The latter used anti-Christian feeling to shore up their position. The local Christians were caught in the crossfire.

The arrival of the Christian missionaries (European and American) and their sponsored schools would serve to further spread Western culture. The minorities were quick to take to the schools and the advantages the missionaries offered. Some of the local Christians converted to Protestantism to profit from the education, protection and the economic opportunities held out by American, British and German missionaries. In the cities of the Fertile Crescent and in Cairo, Jews and Christians seemed overly eager, and far too quick, to abandon their traditional ways of life in favour of newer Western ones. The result of this social upheaval was the further widening of the gap between the Muslim majority and the various minorities who began to be regarded as very likely enemies of the Sultan. 'They were regarded as potential traitors, sources of weakness and instruments of European policy; in general as danger to the empire and to the Islamic community' (Hourani, 1947: 24).

There were, as well, other factors for change which, in Hourani's eyes, fell outside the minorities' control, but which nevertheless served increasingly to isolate them from the rest of the population — the re-Islamization of the Ottoman Empire and the rising flames of nationalism within its boundaries.[2]

In a perhaps futile attempt at self-defence, and to ward off further inroads by the West, the last Ottoman sultans attempted — hopelessly and with unforeseen consequences — to restructure their own state, 'to turn it from a group of loosely connected local, racial and religious units into a military and highly centralized state' (Hourani, 1947: 27). They sought to borrow the technology and military science of the West but not its ideologies. Instead the Ottomans seized upon the ideological power of Islam, with its legacy of past greatness, to provide the empire with its moral willpower and principles. Pan-Islamism was adopted, and by the end of the nineteenth century it set the tone for the empire. Hourani would conclude that this further tore at the fabric of what was once a 'supranational' state and along with it the collective loyalty that the non-Muslim subjects once had for their Sultan.

The increasing reliance on pan-Islamism meant that Christian minorities found themselves more and more alienated. On the other hand, any benefits derived from association with the West would further undermine their position in the eyes of their Muslim neighbours. Geography and political reality could not be eliminated; they could not escape their own world. Thus the yearning for acceptance and a sense of belonging grew to a fever pitch. If the politics of 'pan-Islam'

---

2. For more on this point see the politics of Tanzimat in Chapter 2.

were to draw them apart from the Muslim majority, among whom they lived and shared a common language, land and ancestry, then the 'politics of liberal nationalism' should bring them together and provide a common ground. They believed in a liberal nationalism that would flower under 'the benevolent protection of liberal Europe' and would give rise to a secular Arab nationalism in which Muslims and Christians would be incorporated in exactly the same way (Hourani, 1962a: 277). Hourani recognized the dilemma of secularism: he recognized the difficulty of divorcing Islam, not only as a religion but also as a way of life, from politics. Nevertheless, he was to hold to the view that most Christians are Arab by origin, and most are 'Muslim by culture'. Since Islam was the Arabs' most important contribution to history, the heritage of Islam and its way of life were something that all Arabs, whether Muslim or Christian, can also claim (Hourani, 1947: 30).[3]

Hourani made two decisive qualifications to that sentiment. Though not all Christians embraced nationalism, most Christians of the coastal cities of the Fertile Crescent genuinely considered themselves to be Arab; second, early nationalism was not only the creation of Arab Christians, but was also subscribed to by Muslim Arabs of Syria. In a sense, this nationalism also had an Islamic basis. At that time, at least superficially, there was no great contradiction between

---

3. This point was evident in most of his writings, even as early as the 1947 *Minorities in the Arab World*. The notion of Islamic heritage and culture shared by Arab Christians was, moreover, the theme of what he described to the author as the best essay of his last book, 'T. E. Lawrence and Louis Massignon', in Hourani, 1962: 277.

Islamism and Arabism; both shared the common interest of independence from Ottoman rule:

> The most important of these movements [political movements within the empire in the last 50 years] was Arab nationalism. There is no doubt that the popular force behind the movement in its first phase was Islamic as much as it was Arab; that many of its leaders did not clearly distinguish Islamism from Arabism; and that a very large part of the Arabic-speaking Christians regarded the movement with fear as no more than a scarcely-disguised religious movement. Nevertheless the educated young men who were the real leaders of the movement were in general concerned to preach the separation of politics and religion, and to emphasize the equality of all creeds inside the Arab community; and on that basis they found many collaborators among the Arab Christians, particularly the Greek and Orthodox.
> (Hourani, 1947: 30)

Hourani saw a minority as well as a majority hand in the creation of Arabism. Indeed, he was one of the very few scholars to hold a balanced view on the subject, in that he never overestimated the role Christians played in the intellectual origins of Arab nationalism and nor did he underestimate its Islamic elements. Unlike Antonius, he was careful not to give too much weight to the intellectual contributions of Christian Arabs:[4] unlike Sylvia Haim and Elie Kedourie he did

---

4. See his criticism of Antonius in 'Lebanese Historians and the Formation of a National Image', in Hourani, 1981: 165–6.

not downplay the intellectual role Christian minorities played in the development of Arab nationalism (see Haim, 1962).[5]

Despite his deep-seated liberalism Hourani was not blind to the pressures that modern nationalism and the age of the nation-state would bring to bear on the Christian Arabs and on Muslim-Christian relations. He saw the dangers early on in *Minorities in the Arab World* — published in 1947 — long before the sectarian warfare of Lebanon and the running battles between Islamic extremists and the Copts in Egypt: 'If Arab and Egyptian nationalism should become essentially Islamic movements, giving the Arab Christians at best an inferior position on the margin of the national community, then the status of the religious communities cannot be improved' (Hourani, 1947: 121). The liberal in him trusted in assimilation, the development of a process whereby the Christian is given 'a distinctive place in the national community, and one by no means inferior to that of the Moslem' (Hourani, 1947: 121).

This was, of course, more easily said than done. For this to work, politics would have to remain a process of the elites. The foreign powers would have to stay at bay; the local contenders for power would have to refrain from looking for outside protection. And, as is often the case, in Hourani the tension between Europe's own power in the Levant and the local Muslim-Christian balance is given great importance.

---

5. Her emphasis was that: 'it was possible to see in it [Arab nationalism] the outcome of the severe intellectual crisis that Islam experienced during the nineteenth century, and from which it emerged damaged, enfeebled, no longer a political weapon against European domination' (Haim, 1962: 6).

> If nationalism continues to be primarily a movement of defence against and opposition to the Western Powers it is inevitable that it should regard with suspicion those minorities which share the religious or other characteristics of the West; it is inevitable, too, that some at least of those minorities should be torn between their national and religious loyalties, and that the Western Powers should be tempted to make use of such minorities.
> (Hourani, 1947: 121)

The Christian Arabs, Hourani recognized, could take Arab nationalism only so far. They could set the stage, translate the literature of Europe, spark an intellectual renaissance. But the other principal stream — Muslim modernism — possessed greater force and vision. It had greater self-confidence, and could strike a deal with the West, with modernization, without having to worry about the embrace of Europe. As the Muslim modernists spoke to their people they were intent on saving Islam from the assault of Europe. Islam, they said, had to be changed to withstand the encroachment of the outside world.

As Hourani depicts the Muslim modernists, they were men who for all their professions of faith were politically driven and interested in national power.

> They had all been influenced by the European idea that there is a sphere of religion and a sphere of secular life, and the principles they appealed to were for the reform of secular life and were human, rational ones — individual rights, civilization, social utility.
> ('Middle Eastern Nationalism: Yesterday and Today', in Hourani, 1981: 185)

The Intellectual Origins of Arab Nationalism

They believed that the matter of religion (of Islam) could be finessed, and that secular nationalism would win the day. But nationalism among the peoples of the Middle East, as these men came to learn, could never be wholly secular.

> In the apparently stable countries like Turkey, Egypt and Iran, based on territorial patriotism, there was a submerged religious feeling not coterminous with the nation, which could emerge at moments of crisis.
> ('Middle Eastern Nationalism: Yesterday and Today', in Hourani, 1981: 186–7)

If this held for the Turks and the Iranians, it was truer in the case of the Arabs. As Hourani has so aptly put it:

> Islam was what the Arabs had done in history, and in a sense it had created them, given them unity, law, a culture. For both Muslim and Christian Arabs ... there lay a dilemma at the bottom of Arab nationalism: secularism was necessary as a system of government but how was complete secularism compatible with the existence of an Arab sentiment?
> (Hourani, 1962a: 297)

This insoluble dilemma was to become clearer to the nationalists with the passage of time. For the early Muslim modernists the task was simpler at the beginning. But their contribution was undeniably great. For, as Hourani tells us, the activists Jamal al-Din al-Afghani and Muhammad 'Abduh provided the essential link between a stagnant traditional society and the modern world of nationalism.

It was ironic, perhaps, that the Persian-born Afghani would

play so critical a role in the heritage of Arab nationalism. But the tireless agitator and pamphleteer whose work and travel spanned Iran, India, Egypt and Turkey, was both a relentless anti-imperialist and an ardent Islamic reformer. Hourani's work does not break new ground on Afghani or his mysterious origins. Afghani had claimed an Afghan descent for obvious reasons: he was a Shi'i from Iran but success in the wider world of Islam made it essential for him to claim an Afghan, and Sunni, descent. What we get from Albert Hourani's work is an appreciation of the intellectual role Afghani played in putting down roots that would bear fruit in the years to come:

> In his [Afghani's] political activities, his calls for unity against British aggression, he may seem like a modern nationalist, but there is something also which recalls an older type of political action. He was not a democrat or constitutionalist on principle; what he wanted was rather the typical Islamic combination of a religious reformer and a strong ruler. He was modern, however, in his thought about the direction of reform. Muslims should become part of the modern world, and the modern world had two bases, reason and worldly activity aiming at progress. In his view these were of the essence of the true Islam. ... By returning to the truth of their religion Muslims would acquire the sources of strength in the modern world.
> ('Middle Eastern Nationalism: Yesterday and Today', in Hourani, 1981: 184)

Afghani's disciples, mainly his more conservative and status-quo-oriented follower, the Egyptian Muhammad 'Abduh, built on the intellectual energy that Afghani had introduced. What

The Intellectual Origins of Arab Nationalism

they did, Hourani observes, was to reduce the difference between Islam and other religions ('Middle Eastern Nationalism: Yesterday and Today', in Hourani, 1981: 184–5). Fighting against the power of Europe, 'they opened the way to new and more effective principles drawn from the advanced thought of Europe' ('Middle Eastern Nationalism: Yesterday and Today', in Hourani, 1981: 185).

Thus had pan-Islamism made its contribution to Arab nationalism. Afghani and 'Abduh, men of the nineteenth century, had raised some fundamental questions that younger Muslim Arabs would contend with after the collapse of Ottoman authority and power.

An intellectual historian primarily interested in the development of ideas, Hourani does not tell us much about the 'content' of Arab nationalism, or its social and economic bases. He did not delve into this kind of research. However, he does provide his readers with a general sense of the groups of thinkers, publicists, and officials who were to spearhead Arab nationalism in the interwar years. The fortunes of Arab nationalism had been attached to the Arab revolt of the Sharif Husayn of Mecca and his sons — the Hashemites. In a very insightful passage Hourani sketches the outlook and background of the men who took it upon themselves to lead the Arab national movement:

> They had, whether they were Syrians or Iraqis, a common mind, a system of ideas which formed the political orthodoxy of the years between the wars. First of all, they believed implicitly in the idea of an Arab nation: in schools, in barracks, in the Ottoman parliament in exile in Cairo, and in the Sharifian forces they had come to know each other and acquired the ease

of discourse which possession of a common language and a common education gives.

(Hourani, 1962a: 293)

These nationalists would become more strident as European hegemony set in after the First World War. The mandate system, dominated by Britain and France, would help radicalize the nationalists. Hourani explains the reasons behind this change quite well. Where the Arab countries had been relatively united under Ottoman rule, European domination divided them. Under this division rival ideas and conceptions of identity would emerge — ideas of Iraqi, Lebanese and Syrian nationalism. Much as the nationalists had insisted that these states were only a step toward the reunification of the Arab world, these ideas of smaller nationalisms were there to stay. Greater Syria had its proponents; so did the idea of a separate Lebanese destiny.

We do find in Hourani's work an appreciation of both Greater Syrian and Lebanese nationalisms. Syria and Lebanon were more familiar to him than Egypt and the Arabian Peninsula, their ideas more accessible and immediate. Of the two, Greater Syrian nationalism was to mount a more direct challenge to Arab nationalism in the interwar years. Inspired and led by Antun Sa'ada, a Lebanese Christian brought up in Brazil, a would-be imitator of European fascist politics, the Syrian Social Nationalist Party emerged as a formidable movement in the late 1930s and the 1940s. Sa'ada, an adventurer with a weakness for parades and uniforms and fiery speeches and para-military organizations, had no interest in Arab nationalism. He had held Egypt in contempt, thought it a distant African country, and had no knowledge of the world of the Arabian Peninsula. His political ideas were confined to the

Fertile Crescent and Greater Syria — Syria, Lebanon and Palestine. A troublemaker, Sa'ada was a challenge to the fragile political order in Syria and Lebanon. He was put to death by the Lebanese authorities in 1949. But the ideas he had brought with him when he returned to his ancestral home from the New World would not be easily discarded. Sa'ada tapped the idealism and extremism of a generation that believed that the old order of notables had to be challenged. His belief in the natural frontiers of Greater Syria found a receptive audience. So did his denunciation of the ineptness of the Arab states in their confrontation with the idea of a 'Jewish national home' in Palestine.

In the case of Lebanon and Lebanese nationalism, Arab nationalism was to meet a smaller challenge, but one of longer duration. Hourani gives us the reasons why ideas of Lebanese nationalism would linger. To begin with, these ideas drew their power and their vitality from the country's Maronite community. The Maronites of the mountain were adamant in their insistence that Lebanon had its own form of civilization, 'Christian, Mediterranean, linked with the Latin powers of Europe' (Hourani, 1962a: 319).

Hourani saw Lebanon as 'a paradox', a 'blend of two worlds' (Hourani, 1962a: 321). He understood its fragility, but held out the hope that its democracy and political freedom would save it. Forced to choose between Arab nationalism and the West, Hourani knew Lebanon was bound to come apart. Its survival required an *entente* between the two. But during what Hourani has labelled 'the climax of Arabism' in the 1950s and 1960s, the era dominated by the Egyptian leader Jamal 'Abd al-Nasir, that *entente* could not be reached.

That 'Abd al-Nasir would emerge as the true heir and dominant figure of Arab nationalism shows both the transformation of Arab nationalism and its limits. 'Abd al-Nasir was an Egyptian: Arab nationalism had begun in the Fertile Crescent. He was an officer; the nationalist movement had been born among the intellectuals. But this aside, 'Abd al-Nasir dominated the public life of the Arab countries during a turbulent decade. Whatever its limitation at home, Nasirism, says Hourani, 'met with a vast and continuing public acceptance' (Hourani, 1991a: 407) in other Arab countries.

The 'pretensions and claims of Nasirism went beyond its power', Hourani writes in an apt summation (Hourani, 1991a: 411). The crisis of the Six-Day War of 1967 was to show the weakness at the foundation of the Nasirist edifice. The Egyptians had stumbled into a crisis, and they had not built the military or social bases of a strong state. The illusions of Arab unity and Arab power were badly shaken.

Hourani, who had chronicled an era of British primacy in the Arab countries, would observe an era of American predominance in the 1970s. Not particularly anxious to proclaim the demise of Arab nationalism, he did acknowledge it in what was his last major work, *A History of the Arab Peoples*. He noted the traffic of people and goods across Arab frontiers but could not escape the increasing fragmentation of the Arab world, the trend 'towards difference and even hostility rather than greater union' (Hourani, 1991a: 426).

By the time he, one of the two great advocates of Arab nationalism (Antonius being the other), had to face the troubles of Arab nationalism, more sustained and direct challenges to the concept of nationalism had been issued by younger scholars working with different methodologies and assumptions. The most direct challenge was mounted in the late 1970s and the early 1980s in the work of Fouad Ajami. In 'The End of Pan-Arabism' and in *The Arab Predicament*, Ajami made the case for a *raison d'état* against the wider claims of Arab nationalism (see Ajami, 1978/9 and Ajami, 1981).[6] Ajami's case was straightforward. Setting aside the intellectual history that had suffused Hourani's work, Ajami wrote as a student of international relations, focusing on the state and on political practice. The Six-Day War of 1967, he noted, was the 'Waterloo of pan-Arabism and Arab nationalism'. The boundaries of Arab states, he wrote, had been around for six decades. The existence of these boundaries was not novel, and increasingly their power and legitimacy served to 'keep pan-Arab claims at bay and effectively to claim the loyalty of those within' (Ajami, 'The End of Pan-Arabism', in Farah, 1987: 105). Ajami indicates six broad changes that have altered the balance of power against pan-Arabism and in favour of the state:

- The universalism of pan-Arabism derived to a considerable extent from the universalism of the Ottoman Empire. The universalism, lent to the Arabs by the Ottoman system, now belongs to the past.
- The power of the intellectuals, which had given Arab nationalism its vitality, has waned.
- The anti-colonialism of the mandate years, which traumatized an entire generation, has been replaced by different, more realistic politics.
- The mobile, trans-state elite, which moved from one Arab country to another, has been replaced by a more 'parochial' elite, committed to its own state.

---

6. The debate occasioned by Ajami's 1978/9 article, 'The End of Pan-Arabism', has been brought together in a single book edited by Tawfic Farah (1987).

- The unity forced on the Arabs by the Palestine debacle of 1948 has faded. The Egyptian defection from the Arab stand against Israel fractured that Arab consensus.
- Pan-Arabism had relied on charisma — the charisma of Jamal 'Abd al-Nasir — but the politics of charisma, the world over, has yielded to more practical forms.

A different kind of challenge to Hourani's emphasis on liberal Arab nationalism and its Anglo-French sources was issued by Bassam Tibi, a German-educated scholar, born in Syria, and a member of the faculty of the University of Göttingen. In a book entitled *Arab Nationalism: A Critical Inquiry* (Tibi, 1990), which was published in German in 1971 and translated into English in 1981, Tibi took the study of Arab nationalism in a new direction by emphasizing the importance of its Germanic sources and ideas. These products of the German Romantics had come to the Arab world in the 1920s and 1930s through the work of Sati al-Husri, a very influential publicist and educator (born in 1882) who hailed from a Syrian family of Aleppo. An Ottoman official, Husri made the transition from Ottomanism to Arabism. He played a major role in the development of Iraqi education as director-general of the Ministry of Education and propagated a strongly anti-liberal view of nationalism.

Like the German Romantics, Husri emphasized 'the people' rather than the nation-state. He laid the foundations for fanatical nationalism. Husri dismissed the ideas of French nationalism, which earlier Arab liberals had drawn on. These ideas, Husri maintained, were unsuitable to the Arabs because the Arab world lacked a national bourgeoisie, the group responsible for the creation of the French state and, thus, French nationalism. Husri's emphasis on 'the nation' and 'the people' was, he believed, more suitable to the Arabs. In the German Romantics and their emphasis on 'the spirit' of a nation, and their yearning for emancipation from the French, Husri found a model the Arabs could emulate. Working in Iraq in the 1920s and 1930s, shaping its education, civics courses and history books, Husri was able to come up with a more emotionally satisfying and politically explosive view of nationalism.

The German situation in the world of the nineteenth century — fragmented territory, a single people exalting their idealized past and freedom, looking for a leader to provide them salvation — found a receptive audience in the Arab world. The anti-British and anti-French sentiment in Arab lands gave the German ideas even greater prestige.

By drawing on the German Romantics, and giving Husri his due weight and influence, Tibi was able to provide a historical explanation of the power of models of Arab nationalism in Syria and Iraq that deviated from liberal values. Hourani had paid Husri little attention. He had assumed the liberal character of nationalism, had taken it for granted. Husri had emphasized such powerfully appealing factors as 'language', 'history', 'blood', and 'historical mission'. Tibi reconstructed Husri's sources and explained why his message had the success it did in the interwar years and in the years after. Husri was an authoritarian nationalist and authoritarian nationalism would triumph in key intellectual and political circles in the Arab world. He was intolerant of religious and racial minorities and of the rights of the individual. His crude theories of 'race' and 'the nation' held greater appeal to the crowd and to the military officers than did the restraints of constitutionalism.

What follow are some examples of Husri's formulations — examples that Tibi has selected to demonstrate the appeal of

Husri's theory of nationalism. 'The barracks', Husri observed, 'are as much institutes for national education as the national schools'. Or consider this: 'the struggle for the national awakening requires much more effort and hardship to spread belief in the nation, and all available means must be used to strengthen this belief' (Tibi, 1990: 148). More revealing of Husri's state of mind and of the nationalism he advocated is his idea of what makes a nation:

> A common language and a common history [are] the basis of nation formation and nationalism. The union of these two spheres leads to a union of emotions and aims, sufferings, hope, and culture. Thus the members of one group see themselves as members of a unitary nation, which distinguishes itself from others. However, neither religion nor the state nor a shared economic life are the basic elements of a nation, and nor is common territory. If we want to define the role of language and history for a nation we can say in short that the language is the soul and the life of the nation, but history is its memory and its consciousness.
>
> (Tibi, 1990: 148)

With these views it was not a great surprise that Husri became the ideological teacher for officers in the barracks and for young activists. Tibi persuasively demonstrates how Husri's ideas played a decisive role in shaping modern Arab nationalism. They were politically powerful in Iraq and they came to Syria via the writings and outlook of the founders of the Ba'th Party.

These analyses of pan-Arabism's demise and non-liberal sources stray beyond Hourani's methodology and orientation.

He was a historian of ideas and he was a liberal. He would not accept an analysis that gave such weight to the politics of state at the expense of civilizational analysis. At heart, Hourani was deeply influenced by the work of Arnold Toynbee and his classification of civilizations. He had written when examining Antonius's *The Arab Awakening* that Arnold Toynbee's *The Western Question in Greece and Turkey* was the other book that had shaped the interwar debate on the question of the Middle East ('The Arab Awakening Forty Years Later', in Hourani, 1981: 197–8). More importantly, Hourani had undertaken a major examination of Toynbee's ideas in a lengthy essay entitled 'A Vision of History: An Examination of Professor Toynbee's Ideas' (in Hourani, 1961: 1–34). The essay was not a critique as much as it was a celebration of Toynbee's intellect and contribution in his monumental, six-volume *A Study of History*. Hourani quotes with approval Toynbee's view of the nation-state as a 'prison-house in which our Western souls are incarcerated' ('A Vision of History: An Examination of Professor Toynbee's Ideas', in Hourani, 1961: 2). He echoes Toynbee's warning that we cannot understand a state unless we enlarge our vision to 'include a whole network of them bound together not only by intimate political ties but a common culture and a long tradition of things done and suffered in common' ('A Vision of History: An Examination of Professor Toynbee's Ideas', in Hourani, 1961: 2). It is obvious here that Toynbee's ideas could be easily applied to the Arab world. In other words, to understand a particular Arab state one has to be drawn into the study of Arab civilization.

Hourani resisted the notion that the study of state politics alone could lead to an understanding of the condition of the Arab peoples. It must be remembered that he was the child of Arab immigrants, in Britain, who had grown up with an

exalted, if romantic, idea of the Arab world. He agreed with
Toynbee's notion that 'civilizations were the final entities of
human history' ('A Vision of History: An Examination of
Professor Toynbee's Ideas', in Hourani, 1961: 9). For him, as
he always maintained, the Arab states were too fragile, too
small to stand on their own. There had to be a higher, a larger
notion of identity and the common experience supplied by
Arab nationalism answered that need. 'All Toynbee's concepts
in the end are moral ones,' Hourani writes ('A Vision of
History: An Examination of Professor Toynbee's Ideas', in
Hourani, 1961: 11). That, as well, is a statement on Hourani's
attitude towards politics and nationalism. Were the Arabs to
remain small, feuding states, some rich, the others predominantly poor, the genius of Arab civilization, its special mission,
would never be fulfilled. Even were the Arab states to prove
durable and tenacious, they could not stand for anything above
and beyond the sheer survival of bureaucratic elites.

Like Toynbee, and influenced by him, Hourani was deeply
interested in the historical processes that produced religions.
Given the intimate connection between the Arabs and Islam,
Hourani had to assign Islamic modernism a central place in his
scheme of study. He could not divorce Arabism from Islam or
take the dynastic and republican states of the Arab world as
final units. A larger Arab sensibility, a larger loyalty, gave
shape to the experiences of these divided political entities. The
final chapter of Hourani's *A History of the Arab Peoples*, echoes
the work of Toynbee. Entitled 'A Disturbance of Spirits (since
1967)', it holds out the belief that political ideas are larger,
possess more integrity, than the regimes and governments that
use them. He acknowledges that political ideas grow stale and
become slogans when they are 'appropriated by governments'
(Hourani, 1991a: 454). He knew that Arab nationalism had

suffered that fate, but he could not accept a calculus of power that set civilizational ties aside.

When Saddam Hussein overran Kuwait he did it in the name of Arab nationalism. It is rather interesting to note that Hourani's *A History of the Arab Peoples* only had one single reference to Saddam Hussein, and that in passing. A dictator bent on dominating the Arab world had hijacked Arab nationalism. But none of this would have convinced Hourani that Arab nationalism was a monster that had turned on its creators. His vast output of scholarly work never got bogged down in the details of political events. 'I am not a commentator,' he was to tell the author of this work time and time again. Beyond the squabbles of states, there remains the integral intellectual idea of an Arab nation that the scholar who was shaped by both Manchester and the town of Marjayoun in the south of Lebanon glimpsed when, as a young man, he had come to the land of his ancestors — the land that he saw as a land of Mediterranean sunlight.

4

The Problems of Palestine: The Scholar *Engagé*

It was in 1957, nearly ten years after the loss of Palestine, when Albert Hourani wrote: 'Baudelaire said, the heart has one vintage only. If so, mine will be marked forever by what happened in Palestine' (Hourani, 1957a: 7).[1] Not only was Hourani emotionally committed to the cause of Palestine, but he gave it his best years, the years of his youth and full energy. Following the thread of Hourani's struggle with the problem of Palestine reveals a number of things: he was among the very few Arab scholars who wrote and spoke on the subject of Palestine and he helped to initiate the debate between Arabs and Jews. This was perhaps his most serious contribution to the question of Palestine. Moreover, throughout his writing there are startling predictions of the train of events as well as a genuine critique of himself and the kind of world he once lived in. Under difficult circumstances, and with limited resources, young Hourani gave the Arab case its best defence. University

---

1. During an interview in London on 19 May 1991, Hourani reiterated his conviction that this 35-year-old statement retained its validity.

The Problems of Palestine: The Scholar Engagé

of Texas historian Wm. Roger Louis has pointed out that Hourani was recognized by the advocates of the Zionist cause as their 'most relentless opponent' (Louis, 1984: 413 including footnote number 46).

Hourani's engagement with the Palestinian question began in the late 1930s when he was teaching at the American University of Beirut. On that politically charged campus — an environment where the ideology of Arab nationalism reigned supreme — the question of Palestine was hard to avoid. It was at the centre of political and intellectual life. These were also the years of the Arab rebellion in Palestine — a rebellion that raged between 1936 and 1939. The rebellion was to fail; Palestinian society could not sustain it or provide an answer to British power and to the growing effectiveness of the Zionist movement. But the rebellion in nearby Palestine and the environment of Beirut with its strong currents of Arab nationalism had a lasting influence on the political mind of Albert Hourani.

> At this time I saw the problems of Syria and Palestine in the perspective of Arab nationalism. This was an idea about which I learned in Beirut; that there was an Arab nation of which the emergence to full, independent and united national life was being impeded by British and French rule, and by the artificial frontiers imposed upon it after the First World War, and that if only its energies could be released, it could move into a new and more fruitful period of social and intellectual growth.
> (Hourani, 1991e: 32–3)

The personal background of the scholar could only strengthen this general intellectual outlook. Hourani's ancestors came from the southern part of Lebanon, right by the frontier with northern Palestine. Across that frontier commerce and people had moved for centuries. The idea that the Anglo-French division between a British zone in Palestine and a French zone of influence in Syria and Lebanon was an 'artificial' one came naturally to him.

To his short public career with the Foreign Office Research Department (1939–43) Hourani brought an intense awareness of the stakes involved in Palestine. This could be seen in his first professional report to the Foreign Office. The Arab rebellion had failed; there was a deceptive calm, he warned.

> Since the beginning of the war there has been no major disturbance in Palestine, but this does not mean that the tension has relaxed. The Arabs have remained quiet because of exhaustion after the revolt, the dissolution of their political organizations, the partial stoppage of the flow of Jewish immigration and of land-sales in accordance with the White Paper, and finally their desire not to embarrass Great Britain. They still remain firm however in their insistence that Palestine shall remain an Arab country; as a first step they would be willing to accept the White Paper or some similar measure. Almost all sections of the Zionists have now come out openly in favour of the establishment of a Jewish State in Palestine: some still hope to obtain it through the support of Great Powers, others believe that the Jews must achieve it by their own efforts — hence the purchase of arms, the formation of para-military organizations and the terrorist activities. The British government is trying to find a compromise between these two parties, but in reality it has already found the only possible compromise. The

White Paper demands sacrifices from both sides: the Arabs must recognize the position of the half million Jews already in the country, the Jews must be satisfied with what they have and look elsewhere for a solution of the problem of European Jewry. The Zionists would never accept the White Paper officially, but many of them would acquiesce if it were carried out firmly. The Arabs would certainly revolt, with the assistance of the Arab States, if a Jewish State were established, but if the White Paper were fully carried out they would lose their fear both of Zionism and of the British government's intentions.

(Hourani, 1946a: 38)

In his long second report, he warned the British of the consequences of a policy that fails to stop further Jewish immigration and to prevent the establishment of a Jewish state in Palestine:

A book on Arab affairs may be pardoned for emphasizing one point which has hitherto been ignored in most discussions of the Palestinian situation: that in addition to a world Jewish problem there is a world Arab problem. It is not simply a question of avoiding injustice or granting compensation to a million peasants in Palestine, it is a question of ... what part it will play in the world. ... The alternatives which lie before the Arabs have been defined: they are those of communion with the West and of excommunication from it. Nothing is so likely to drive the Arabs to make the wrong choice as the continuation of a Zionist policy which they regard as unjust. It cannot fail to arouse in the Arabs, as it would in any nation similarly placed, strong hostility both towards the Jews and the Western States.

(Hourani, 1946b: 272–3)

This report was later published as a book under the title *Syria and Lebanon*, and in its preface Hourani was to concede that there were 'certain defects' (Hourani, 1946b: vii) in his work. The report had been written in wartime, in a rapidly changing world. It was hard to make long-range predictions and to recommend policies that would stand the test of time. For one, Hourani had taken it for granted that the Arab states would be willing to accept the White Paper the British had issued in 1939 with the aim of limiting Jewish immigration to Palestine to 75,000 and making further immigration contingent on Arab acceptance. But the Arab states — and the Palestinian leadership — rejected the White Paper. More importantly, Hourani had overestimated the ability of the Arab states to bring the Zionist enterprise in Palestine to a halt. A quarter-century after the Balfour Declaration the Zionist movement had put down roots; the Arab states were in no position to overturn the status quo. Hourani had made the classic appeal to justice, to the future estrangement of the Arab world from Britain. But the discrepancy of power between the Zionists and the Palestinians would overwhelm such appeals.

By the end of 1945 Hourani was to leave the world of research in the Foreign Office and to opt for a deeper engagement with the Palestinian affair. He joined the Arab Office, a newly created organization, which the Arab League had set up and whose financing came from the Iraqi government of Nuri al-Said. The major objective of the Arab Office was the promotion of the Palestinian cause. It had three principal centres of activity: London, Washington and Jerusalem. Albert

The Problems of Palestine: The Scholar Engagé

Hourani, working out of its Jerusalem office, was to be its principal writer and researcher: his brother, Cecil Hourani, directed the Washington branch. The Arab Office was to be a short-lived affair, inevitably doomed to failure. But its intellectual output, bearing the heavy imprint of Hourani, was a major phase in the scholar's life and formation.

It was a remarkable Palestinian political figure by the name of Musa Alami who headed the Arab Office and exerted a strong and lasting influence on Hourani's commitment to the cause of the Palestinians. Years later, Hourani was to describe Alami as 'the most intelligent and responsible of the Palestinian leaders' (Hourani, 1962a: 355).

Cambridge-educated, enlightened, free of any trace of hatred of Jews, Alami was at the centre of a web of friendships with a large number of British officials and Zionist and Jewish leaders. Where other Palestinian leaders had chosen in the late 1930s to cultivate relations with Nazi Germany, Musa Alami had kept his distance and retained his ties to the British. He was thus in a good position in the mid-1940s to serve as an advocate of his people's cause. The Arab Office he led, and which Hourani joined, was a body of liberal advocacy. Alami, Albert and Cecil Hourani and others who had joined this enterprise were men with a common educational and cultural outlook. They were Western-educated; they admired British political institutions and culture. For them, the struggle for Palestine was to decide Britain's standing in the eyes of the Arabs.

Alami was through and through a believer in pan-Arabism. If there were to be a solution for the Palestinians, Alami was sure that the salvation had to come from the Arab states. Alami was scornful of the Arab governments, of their verbal support for the Palestinians, while the Jews were busy building schools and clearing the land. Left alone, the Palestinians were sure to lose the uneven race with the Zionists, Alami was sure. The only remedy was the deeper involvement of the Arab states around Palestine. Writing in 1962, Hourani summed up Alami's outlook:

> Musa Alami was the only Palestinian Arab leader who had an answer to this situation. The theoretical answer he gave in a famous book, *The Lesson of Palestine*, in which, while not absolving England from her share of the blame for the tragedy, he pointed out that it would not have happened but for weaknesses in the regimes and society of the Arab countries.
> (Hourani, 1962b: 319–22)

We owe to Cecil Hourani an appreciation of the political climate in which the Arab Office was born in 1946. The air was full of optimism and enthusiasm, Europe had come out exhausted from the war, and a new hope was invested in the United States of America, which had begun to play the dominant role in Middle Eastern affairs. It was the high tide of liberal internationalism. The newly created United Nations embodied the ideal of a peaceful international order. Zionist and Arab advocates could still meet and talk face to face then. It was easy for those involved in the Arab Office to believe that their work would yield dividends for the Palestinians and that the fate of the contested land would not be determined by force (Cecil Hourani, 1984: 52–3).

The temperament reflected through the work of the Arab Office was liberal and reasoned; its audience was clearly Western. Most (but not all) of the major publications were written by Albert Hourani. In one of his first works written for the Arab Office entitled *Is Zionism the Solution of the Jewish*

The Problems of Palestine: The Scholar Engagé 113

Problem?, Hourani sets out to do battle with Zionism's *raison d'être*, the belief that the situation of the Jews — unique in the world of nations — required a Jewish state:

> A superficial view [of the Jewish problem] would be that it is simply a question of some thousands or millions of individuals who do not wish to or are unable to live in the countries where they are at present to be found, because of temporary political and social conditions, and for whom some other place of residence should therefore be provided, where they can live more happily and safely than at present. ... The Jewish problem however is much more complicated than this. It is the problem of a group whose members, differing as they do in many respects, are yet united to one another by profound ties of emotion and the spirit, and which has excited and still excites the distrust, suspicion or at least bewilderment of the peoples among whom it lives.
>
> (Hourani, 1946c: 1)

At the root of the Jewish unease in the modern world, Hourani the political advocate saw a deeper problem, and one that the creation of a Jewish state was incapable of resolving: the Jews possessed a sense of mission, of bearing witness to God before the nations, but the Gentile world has never been able to accept this Jewish sense of mission.

> This consciousness of mission, and the rejection of it by the Gentile world, persist in changed forms even among those who have cut themselves loose from traditional Judaism, Christianity or Islam. This is the fundamental cause of the abnormality of the Jews, and of their failure

to enter into full communion with any of the peoples among whom they dwell and establish a normal moral relationship with them, that is to say a relationship of trust, respect, and the recognition of equality.

(Hourani, 1946c: 4)

Create a Jewish state and the unease of the Jews in the modern world would persist: the state would offer no solution to this dilemma. Assimilation into the world of nations was the better answer. Such was Hourani's starting point, clearly a position at odds with the very bases of modern Zionism. Mainstream Zionism had settled on Palestine as the place that would redeem Jewish history and arouse Jewish enthusiasm after the calamities of the Holocaust. Hourani took issue with this central tenet as well:

Will not the idea of saving the European Jews from further privation and giving them the possibility of a new life be sufficient to generate enthusiasm? Until the imposition of severe restrictions upon entry into the United States, many more Jews emigrated to America than to Palestine; did they work with less enthusiasm or success in building their new life in America than their brothers in Zion.

(Hourani, 1946c: 9)

Around the corner Hourani could see the looming threat. Palestine was not a vacant land, he observed. True, the Jewish national movement had built some nascent structures in the 1920s and 1930s. But the declaration of a Jewish state, he warned, would put a good deal of what the Jews built at risk: the whole region would turn against the Jewish presence and the goodwill needed to safeguard the Jewish community would be sure to evaporate:

> Nothing is so likely to endanger what the Jews have already achieved in Palestine as the attempt to establish a Jewish state there. The Jews have built up in Palestine a large and well-organized community, have saved half-a-million individuals from massacre in Europe and have revived the Hebrew language and culture. What has been created can only be safeguarded through friendly relations with the Arabs; to attempt to expand it is to incur the certain and permanent enmity of the Arabs inside and outside Palestine, and thus to bring the whole structure into danger. The fact that the Jews have already created something of value in Palestine is thus not a reason for attempting to establish a Jewish State in Palestine, but rather a reason against attempting anything so foolish and dangerous.
> (Hourani, 1946c: 10)

Hourani was to return full circle to what he saw as the only viable solution to the 'Jewish question': assimilation. The Jews were better served, he wrote, if they were to take advantage of the spread of democratic ideas in Europe. It was in those societies, and on the other side of the Atlantic, in the United States, that the solution to the Jewish question was to be found.

The work of the Arab Office had given the scholar a political arena and a political voice. His next assignment, perhaps his most important one in Palestinian affairs, was his contribution to the Anglo-American Committee of Inquiry. Established in 1946, the main objective of the committee was to examine the political, social, and economic possibilities of a settlement in Palestine for those Jews in Europe who were victims of Nazi and Fascist persecution, and to hear the views of competent witnesses from the Arab and Jewish sides (for the full text of the committee report see Anglo-American Committee of Inquiry, 1946). Although the committee's recommendation for a bi-national state was rejected, it was still a very important one for three reasons that Hourani later offered:

> First, it marked the first attempt by the British new Labour government, at that time, to think through the problem as to what should be done. Second, it was the first official intervention by the government of the United States as the inheritor of British power in the Middle East and in the affairs of Palestine. Third, by the end of the hearing, all members of the committee came to the conclusion that there will never be peace in Palestine without Arab participation.
> (Interview with Hourani, London, 7 May 1991)

Hourani appeared before the committee as a representative of the Arab Office lobbying for the establishment of Palestine as a self-governing state with an Arab majority, with full rights for its Jewish citizens. His testimony before the committee was a short but carefully prepared pamphlet entitled *The Problem of Palestine*. Though a work of political advocacy, it had great analytical power. He drove his points home and dissected such crucial matters as the ties between Palestine and Greater Syria and the larger Arab nation, the case for an independent Arab-ruled Palestine, and the folly of attempting to impose a Jewish state in Palestine (Arab Office, Washington DC, 1946).[2] To the 12 British and American members of the committee, he put the Arab case with conviction but with reason.[3] It was something that he and Alami took seriously. He sought to underline to the committee the Arab opposition to the entire Zionist scheme:

> I think it is right to emphasize, without elaborating what needs no further elaboration, the unalterable opposition of the Arab nation to the attempt to impose a Jewish state upon it. This opposition is based upon the unwavering conviction of unshakable rights and a conviction of the injustice of forcing a long-settled population to accept immigrants without its consent being asked and against its known and expressed will — the injustice of turning a majority into a minority in its own country — the injustice of withholding self-government until the Zionists are in the majority and able to profit by it. The opposition is based also upon the situation of the dangers of Zionism which threatens to distort the whole natural development of Arab peace — social, economic, political, and intellectual — and

---

2. The 15-page report is quite significant. It became the basis for a more elaborate report entitled *The Future of Palestine*.
3. During an interview with Hourani, London, 6 May 1991, Hourani expressed to the author his discontent with the manner in which Ahmed Shuqairi conducted his presentation before the committee. According to Hourani, Shuqairi's testimony was explosive, his voice was very loud and he threatened many times that the Arabs would use violence. Later, the Arab League appointed Shuqairi to head the newly-created Palestine Liberation Organization. For Shuqairi's testimony, see Anglo-American Committee of Inquiry, 1946, 25 March, 123–30.

threatens also if not to dominate the Arab world, at least to disturb its life for generations to come.

(Anglo-American Committee of Inquiry, 1946: 131)[4]

In Hourani's brief, partition, a bi-national state, and the perpetuation of the status quo, were three 'illusory' solutions which different witnesses from the Zionist side had put before the committee. He foresaw the troubles of partition with some clarity:

> Partition would be opposed to the very object of peace, and that for two reasons. First, because it is clear that the establishment of a Jewish state in part of Palestine would not satisfy the great majority of Zionists who want political domination over the whole of Palestine, at least. If they obtain a state in part of Palestine, they would be tempted to use it as the first step to pressing further claims. The establishment of a Jewish State in part of Palestine would not satisfy them, but would strengthen their position and encourage them to ask for more. That, on the one hand. On the other hand, even if they accepted partition in the first place, there are factors at work which would draw them, sooner or later, and probably sooner, into inevitable conflict with the surrounding Arab world. There is a dynamic force in Zionism which, unless it is checked now, will lead them on to destruction. They will be forced into conflict with the Arab world by various factors; by the need to deal with their own Arab minority, who would not consent

---

4. A copy was provided by Hourani during an interview with the author in London, 13 May 1991.

The Problems of Palestine: The Scholar Engagé

> willingly to become the subjects of a Jewish state and who would rise and protest and whose protest would be aided actively by surrounding Arab countries, so that for reasons of internal security and in order to deal with their minority, the Jewish State would be brought into conflict with the surrounding countries. Then again, in certain circumstances, I can imagine the pressures of population in the Jewish State would be so great it would turn the thoughts of the governing body to expansion, either in order to settle Jewish immigrants outside the Jewish State, or else in order to evacuate their Arab minority. Also in certain circumstances, they might be led to expansion by the need to secure stable markets for their industrial products.
> (Anglo-American Committee of Inquiry, 1946: 133–4)

Nor did a bi-national state promise a solution to the acute struggle between Arab and Jew, he was to argue. In the Palestine of the 1940s, a bi-national state was utopian. The two national groups were radically different: the minority (the Jews) would use the machinery of the state to achieve its own goals, and the two nationalities would be doomed to perpetual strife.

The status quo — British rule in Palestine — was not much better than the other alternatives. In Hourani's view, the mandatory government would find itself doing the bidding of the Zionists. This was precisely what the Zionists desired, he observed. 'Nothing suits the Zionists so much as a situation in which the task of repressing and coercing the Arabs is undertaken by a foreign government, or by an international organization while the flow of Jewish immigration continues uninterrupted' (Anglo-American Committee of Inquiry, 1946:

135) In sum, the extension of the mandate would not provide a radical change in the situation or do anything to solve the problem; on the contrary, things would worsen and the matter would become more complicated.

Hourani was to put before the committee a theme that would become the centrepiece of Arab liberalism's contention on the matter of Palestine. The fate of Palestine was, to him, a test case of the ability of the Arab world to come to terms with the West. Thwarted in Palestine, he was sure, the Arabs would turn away from the West.

> It seems clear to me that the main task of the Arabs today is to come to terms with Western civilization and with the new Westernized world community which is coming into existence, and the Arabs are faced today with a choice between paths: either they can go out towards the West and towards the world in openness and receptiveness, trying to take from the West what is of most value and greatest depth in its tradition and blend it with what they have of their own, trying to establish a relationship of tolerance and trust between them and the Western nations with whom they are brought into contact, and trying to enter into the new world community on a level of equality and in a spirit of cooperation; or else they can turn away from the West and from the world, in spiritual isolation and in hatred, taking nothing from the outside world except the material means with which to combat it. I believe the first path is the path that the Arabs must follow, and that the responsible leaders among them want to follow. Nevertheless, the attitude which the Arabs will take up towards the West is not entirely a matter for the Arabs

The Problems of Palestine: The Scholar Engagé   121

themselves; it depends very largely upon the attitude which the West takes up towards them, and it is at this point that Zionism comes in.
(Anglo-American Committee of Inquiry, 1946: 45)

Bartley Crum, an American member of the committee, thought that Hourani gave the Arab case its 'most competent summation' (Crum, 1947: 254). In an exchange with the committee, Hourani was pressed as to whether an Arab world imbued with a newly released sense of nationalism could assure the Jews fair treatment. There were 'great risks' involved, he said, 'but I do not despair'. The Arab proposals, he argued, were the only ones that 'offer the slightest chance of avoiding some dreadful catastrophe to the country' (Crum, 1947: 256–7).

The main recommendation of the Anglo-American Committee called for:

- the establishment of a bi-national state that neither Arab nor Jew would dominate;
- the extension of the British mandate until the animosity between the Arabs and the Jews came to an end; and
- the immediate admission of 100,000 Jews from Europe to Palestine.

The work of the committee was soon overtaken by events. By mid–1947 Britain had decided to rid itself of the responsibility for Palestine and to turn the issue over to the United Nations. The Arab League and the Palestinian leadership represented by Hajj Amin Husseini, the Mufti of Jerusalem, decided to boycott the work of the United Nations and that of its newly created body, the Special Committee on Palestine (UNSCOP). The publicists of the Arab Office faced a dilemma, outlined by Cecil Hourani:

> To assume beforehand that the new committee would be prejudiced in favour of the Zionist point of view and to refuse to talk with it would mean that the Zionists would have the field to themselves, and the Arab case would go by default. On the other hand, to go against the decision of the higher Committee and against the decision of the Arab governments and the Arab League was difficult, and might even be dangerous.
> (Cecil Hourani, 1984: 68–9)

The Arab Office decided to limit its participation to the submission of its earlier report now expanded and entitled *The Future of Palestine*. Written by Albert Hourani, this was to be the Arab Office's best single document (Arab Office, London, 1947).[5] Its main thesis was a presentation of the Arab case against partition; its pages have the most powerful defence ever of the Arab case in Palestine. But it was too late for that: on 29 November 1947, the General Assembly of the United Nations voted in favour of the partition of Palestine. The words of Cecil Hourani convey the feeling of those who had taken part in the work of the last few years:

---

5. The book appeared under anonymous authorship, but it was mainly written by Albert Hourani with Musa Alami participating in the political analysis and Charles Issawi contributing to the economic aspects. Albert Hourani conveyed this during an interview with him in London on 6 May 1991.

> As I sat with my colleagues in the Arab Office and friends from the Arab delegations while the final stages of the General Assembly's discussions were being held, an atmosphere of almost unbearable tension built up. We were all conscious, I think, that history was being made, but until the final vote was taken the outcome was uncertain. When it was announced, the scene which followed has been forever engraved on my memory: the jubilation of the Zionist delegation and the emotional congratulations they received from both the American and Russian delegates, and the slow march of the Arab delegations led by Emir Faisal as they walked out of the General Assembly in protest both at the decision and the way it had been taken.
>
> (Cecil Hourani, 1984: 70)

The Arab Office was shut down before the protagonists took to the battlefield in 1948. For Albert Hourani, it was time to go back to the world of teaching and scholarship at Oxford. He had done what he could for a cause that gripped him. He brought to his writings on Palestine the experience of the Arab Office. The lessons of that experience were to be seen in his writings of the 1950s on this issue. To the Anglo-American Committee he had described the struggle for Palestine in moral terms: 'Ultimately this is not a political or an economic problem to be decided only by political or economic criteria; ultimately and inescapably it is a moral question' (Anglo-American Committee of Inquiry, 1946: 143). This was to remain his central theme on this issue, the cornerstone of his work. In Hourani's final verdict there was enough blame to go around: the Arabs had not acquitted themselves well in Palestine, nor had Britain. In large part, Hourani accepted that the Arabs were responsible for their defeat in the war of 1948. Those who supported the Arabs overestimated Arab capability to translate words to deeds. In the military sphere their methods were archaic. There was no central command or unified action. Their military defeat was the result of Arab disunity and political weakness. Influenced by Musa Alami's self-critique of the 1948 defeat, Hourani wrote: 'the Arab governments have failed to give the ordinary people some stake in the country, some positive good which is worth defending; and the Arab people are lacking in political consciousness' (Hourani, 1949: 135).

But Great Britain was partly to blame and bears a moral responsibility. The establishment of a Jewish national home in Palestine was a policy that Britain deliberately adopted. Throughout 30 years in Palestine, Great Britain had not only maintained the status quo, but had also planted the seed of future troubles. Jewish immigration was permitted until the number of Jews in Palestine approximated a third of the total of its Arab population. Furthermore, throughout the troubles of 1936–39, Great Britain undertook actions to demolish Arab resistance but never did the same to the Zionist forces. By the time British forces had destroyed the Arab rebellion of 1936–39, the outcome of the struggle between the Palestinians and the Zionists had been all but determined.

Hourani saw British policy up close and understood it well. Britain was caught between conflicting currents. British officials, he observed, had not on the whole been supportive of Zionism. They 'knew the reality of the problem, and were unwilling to hold the Arabs by force until the Jews should be strong enough to dominate or expel them' (Hourani, 1953b: 162). Furthermore, they understood the need to maintain the friendship and goodwill and strategic cooperation of the Arab states. But other forces were at play. As Hourani describes it, the Zionists had the edge when it came to political sophistication and experience in world politics. Compared with the Zionist diplomatists, the Arab players were parochial politicians with little knowledge of the world beyond.

He had no illusions about the bureaucratic working of a large imperial government: he wrote of the 'tendency of governments not to make up their minds until decisions can no longer be avoided, and then to decide in accordance with the balance of forces at that moment' (Hourani, 1953b: 15). Britain in Palestine had given a stark display of this kind of ambivalence and indecision.

Two decades later, following the Six-Day War of 1967, Hourani was to revisit his old Palestinian themes in an exchange with the distinguished Israeli historian J. L. Talmon in the *Observer*. The problem had become more acute; more Palestinians had been driven into exile, large numbers had come under Israeli rule. He lamented the uneven way the West viewed the rights of the Israelis and those of the Palestinians:

> It seemed to most Arabs that Western governments talked in one way about the rights of the Jews, and in another about those of the Arabs. They often said that Israel was here to stay; they never said the Palestinian Arab nation was here to stay. They talked in language of high principles and threats about Israel's right to free navigation; they used a milder language about the right of the refugees to return or compensation. Unwise statements by Arab spokesmen about throwing Israel into the sea were widely quoted and condemned; no one

seemed to care that Israel had, in fact, thrown a large number of Arabs into the desert.

(Hourani and Talmon, 1967: 11)[6]

Hourani saw Israel perched between two possibilities: one of having peace with the Arabs but on her own terms, the other of war with the Arabs, which might give it better frontiers. The humane and viable way out for Israel was to accept the responsibility for the Palestinians who lived under its control and to give the refugees the right to return to their lands or to compensate them. He was pessimistic. With clarity, he foresaw some of what was to haunt Israel two decades later with the eruption of the *intifada*.

It seems more likely than not that Israel will do nothing. If so, it may stay in Gaza and the West Bank; part of the Arab population may be squeezed out; the rump of Jordan may be absorbed into some other state; and in a few more years the Palestinian Arab nation may rise once more to haunt Israel, this time inside as well as outside its frontiers.

(Hourani and Talmon, 1967: 15)

---

6. In an interview with Hourani in Washington, DC on 10 May 1989, Hourani explained the reason for writing this piece and for the exchange with Talmon. He said that David Astor — who was the owner and editor of the *Observer* — had insisted that, due to the spreading dominance of Zionist propaganda after the Six-Day War, it was urgent that someone write effectively from the Arab point of view. Thus, Hourani agreed to make an exception and write his article, which appeared together with that of Talmon in book form.

The Problems of Palestine: The Scholar Engagé

In this exchange, and in everything he wrote before on the Palestinian issue, Hourani was both a lawyer with a good brief for his client, and a moralist. He knew the weakness and the errors of the Palestinian leadership, but he saved his ammunition and his fire for the Western powers, the Zionists and the Arab state. The Palestinians were the losers, he said. To criticize them was 'like kicking a man when he is down' (interview with Hourani, 6 May 1991). The cause of his youth was never abandoned.

In a text written as the fight for Palestine was approaching its decisive outcome, Hourani had defined the centrality of the Palestinian question to the encounter between the Arabs and the West. He had written that Palestine would decide whether there would be an Arab 'communion' with the West or 'excommunication' from it (Hourani, 1946b: 272–3). 'Communion' and 'excommunication' are, of course, religious terms. This conveys the depth of Hourani's commitment to the question of Palestine. For him — as it was for others of his Western-educated generation — there was a strong belief that the future of Palestine would decide the fate of Arab liberalism, and the nature of the bonds between the Arabs and the West. Hourani's fear was that the British betrayal over Palestine would embitter future generations of Arabs and turn them away from Britain and Western values.

On Palestine, Hourani was an activist engaged. His language gives away the depth of his passion. How else can a reader explain the passage from Baudelaire about the heart having one vintage only, and terms like 'communion' and 'excommunication?' Many things must have gone into Hourani's engagement with the Arab Office and the issue of Palestine: his loyalty to his ancestors (Marjayoun, the village from which his family came was right on the border with northern Palestine);

his desire to square his British loyalty with service to the Arabs; his hope for a viable liberalism. As the events of 1948 in Palestine were to demonstrate, all these hopes were to be denied.

5

Lebanon: The Pull of the Ancestors

When Albert Hourani, the son of Christian Lebanese emigrants, wrote about Lebanon, he wrote with a certain love and compassion. After all, Lebanon was the dearest place to his heart, the land of his ancestors and of the full sunlight.

> Those years in Beirut were decisive in more than one way. They gave me my first experience of Mediterranean sunlight, after the half-light of the north of England. It was important to know my extended family, or rather my two families, those of my father and mother. I learnt something about myself, and also about the nature of family ties in the Mediterranean world: the way in which ties of blood or connection could give a depth and solidity to all kinds of human relationship, and the values of honour and shame about which social anthropologists were to write so much later.
>
> (Hourani, 1991e: 31)

It was during these years that the young Hourani assumed a teaching position at the American University in Beirut and was able to observe and discern what was going on in Lebanon as well as in other parts of the Middle East.

According to Albert Hourani, the account of a journey that his brother Cecil took in 1939 to Marjayoun — the ancestral family village — is a good reflection of his own attachment to Lebanon (interview with Hourani, London, 12 May 1991). With its crossroads location, Marjayoun has always been an area traversed and fought over by raiders and invaders. For Cecil, his trip was

> a journey back into time, to discover for myself the landscape of my parents' home and the society in which they had grown up. There was therefore from the beginning an *ambiguity* about my attitude which found its reflection in the attitudes even of some members of my own family toward me: was I coming as an Englishman looking for ways to serve the country of his birth, or was I a Lebanese looking for his roots? The truth was that I was both, but this was not easy for everyone to believe. It took me many years before I could resolve the duality in my own mind, and reconcile the loyalties of my divided self.
>
> (Cecil Hourani, 1984: 28, my emphasis)

The Houranis had vivid childhood memories connected with Lebanon. Thanks to their father's nostalgic tales of the homeland and to the heavy traffic of Lebanese visitors and relatives through their Manchester home, Fadlo Hourani's sons kept a vivid picture of Lebanon in their minds. The passion of Marjayoun's inhabitants, the town's rhythm of life and its geography, and the ownership of a family house there made a deep impression on Cecil's, as well as Albert's heart. Coming from the chilly and foggy climate of Manchester, in Marjayoun Cecil was struck by the warmth of human relations. The people's love, generosity, and way of life captured his imagination and changed his perception of belonging:

> What they had all in common was a total devotion to each other, and on the part of my aunts limitless admiration and love for my father amounting to adoration, so that I had to live up to their expectations of what the son of their brother must be. My appearance, my every gesture and movement were watched and interpreted; one consequence was that I could not refuse the food which was heaped on my plate, because I was told that one should eat as much as one loves, and this was the only way I could reciprocate some of the affection they were showing me.
> (Cecil Hourani, 1984: 30)[1]

Besides the human side of the story, there were other aspects of life that fascinated the visitor from Manchester. Cecil's words best describe his own infatuation:

> I could sit on the balcony of our house in the rocking-chair of my grandmother and look as she had, and my father too, at the daily ritual of the sun's appearance over the top of Hermon; I could visit my mother's house in

---

1. In this connection, my memory carries me back to the dinner I had on 12 May 1991 with Albert Hourani and his wife at their home in London. Throughout he kept insisting that I have more and more food.

the village not far away and visualize the life of that large family ruled by my grandfather whose grave still lies in its now-deserted garden. And I could go on a Tuesday — as I still do — to Souk al Khan, the outdoor market for the villages of Wadi Teym, the Arqoub and Marjayoun, and eat grilled meat on the very same stones my father used a hundred years ago, and the ice-cream of Hasbaya made from goats' milk.

(Cecil Hourani, 1984: 31)

Cecil made it clear that the introduction of the Hourani children to the human and physical elements of their parents' homeland was the best lesson in the process of self-knowledge.

The aim here is to present an account of the development of Albert Hourani's own view of Lebanon as a political society. In the period from 1939 to 1943, during his tenure at a research organization established by the Royal Institute of International Affairs at the request of the Foreign Office (later to become the Foreign Office Research Department), Hourani wrote a long report on the question of post-Second World War independence for Syria and Lebanon.[2] His report played a significant role in influencing the recommendation of a secret assessment within the British government that argued that Syria and Lebanon were viable and mature enough to take care of their own domestic as well as national affairs (Louis, 1984: 156–7). Hourani was the first scholar in modern Middle Eastern studies to display a deep sense of understanding of contemporary Lebanon. He went beyond political narrative and provided

---

2. This report was the basis of Hourani's first book, *Syria and Lebanon: A Political Essay*.

original and extensive analyses of the psyche of the different communities of Lebanon. He imbued work on Lebanon and its 'compact communities' with subtlety and affection. The craft readily reveals the intimacy between the historian and his subject. Of that intimacy, he was to write, 'The history of Lebanon, like that of Iceland, will not have many lovers, but those who have once been attracted by it are enthralled forever' (Hourani, 1960: 395–6). Here, we are dealing with a subject Hourani knew well and with which he felt more comfortable. Aside from his personal attachments to Lebanon, there was something about the characteristics of the country's polity that moved Hourani's imagination:

> Lebanon can be of interest to the historian or political scientist because he can see there with peculiar clarity the development of a political society: that is to say, a system of customs and agreements defining the ways in which power should be exercised and neighbours deal with one another.
> ('Lebanon: The Development of a Political Society', in Hourani, 1981: 124)

Lebanon was the quintessential land of minorities; it was natural for a historian who was himself the product of multiple cultures to be drawn to it:

> The history of Lebanon is not, however, that of the expansion of a single community and its political ideas, but that of an uneasy amalgamation of at least four major components, each with its own inherited political culture, and unless Lebanon can accommodate not only their interests but the beliefs about how people should

live together and how power becomes legitimate authority, it will not be a civil society in the full sense.
(Hourani, 1988: 7)

Hourani's historical narrative on Lebanon begins with an account of the *imara* (princedom): it is a long view of history that takes us to the beginning of Mount Lebanon's development as a political society. Prior to the *imara*, the history of that fragment of Bilad al-Sham was the fragmented local history of its religious communities and of their local lords. The neighbouring coastal cities — Beirut, Sayda and Tripoli — were cities of Sunni Islam; in Mount Lebanon and in the province of Jabal Amil, today south Lebanon, the dominant communities were the Druze, the Maronite and the Shi'i. Yet, none of these religious communities was ever a clear demographic majority and none attained hegemony over the others. In Lebanon, the history of the struggle for power was mostly between Maronite lords and Druze princes. No cohesiveness or unity ever existed between the Druzes, Maronites and Shi'is. Essentially, the Ottomans never had direct rule over Lebanon, preferring to leave local lords to handle their own affairs. In the period from 1590 to 1711, the situation changed, however: for the first time, a ruling institution had emerged — the *imara* — which was the product of one group having supremacy over all the others. It is Hourani's contention that the Ma'n and later the Shihab dynasties established the foundation for the future nation-state of Lebanon:

It was the Ma'ni Fakhr al-Din II (1590–1635) who first created a close and permanent union of a number of hitherto separate lordships, and gave them a leadership which most of them recognized and which had at its disposal a standing army and some kind of regular administration. He did not, it is true, establish the Lebanese state as we know it today, but he created the political institution around which Lebanon would eventually crystallise.

('Lebanon: The Development of a Political Society', in Hourani, 1981: 127)

There ensued a tug-of-war between the imperial Ottoman centre and the ruling princes of Mount Lebanon. A greater measure of independence came to the princedom in the early years of the eighteenth century. The leadership provided by the princedom and the state's ability to stand above sectarian differences came to an end in 1842, when the Maronites revolted against Shihab rule ('Lebanon: The Development of a Political Society', in Hourani, 1981: 133). The basis of the princedom's power in large part rested on the ability of the prince to play one group against another; thus the prince was the source of political stability but not of social solidarity. Four important developments resulted from the princedom's demise:

- the secular unity vested in the princedom was destroyed;
- the hierarchy and order of the landed families was loosened;
- there was a rise in religious and communal feeling and long-standing divisions between these communities became even sharper; and
- the events of the 1840s opened the door to outside involvement in the affairs of Lebanon.

The immediate results of the absence of a legitimate authority, however, were the crises of 1858–60: the peasant revolt in

Kisrawan, the communal war of 1860, and the fighting between Christians and Muslims in Damascus ('Lebanon: The Development of a Political Society', in Hourani, 1981: 134).

After the massacres of the Christians in the Druze *qa'immaqamiyya* (administrative district) in 1860, the Ottomans and the French intervened militarily to put an end to the fighting. Also, representatives of the major powers convened in Beirut to inaugurate the reorganization of Mount Lebanon as a political entity of distinctive status within the Ottoman order. Under the protection of the European powers, Lebanon was to become a privileged Ottoman *sanjaq* (district) governed by a Christian *mutasarrif* from outside Lebanon ('Lebanon: The Development of a Political Society', in Hourani, 1981: 134). The order to emerge from this arrangement was to provide equality for all communities, but with a special role for the Maronites. A major change in the balance of power between Europeans and the Ottomans had taken place. The Europeans were now taking more and more interest in the Middle East; Britain was exporting Lancashire cottons, and France had her historic ties with the Maronites and growing commercial interest in the silk industry of Mount Lebanon. The *mutasarrifiyya*, or *sanjaq* system, functioned as a source of order, but it planted the seeds of future trouble. A historian with a long view could see the mixed blessing of what the European powers had done:

> The arrangement of 1861 once more provided a framework of authority within which the life of Lebanon could develop, but at a price: it widened the gap between the districts inside the framework and those outside. Inside the *sanjaq*, there developed a peasant society of small freeholders cultivating silk for the European market, and

> a separate political consciousness, moulded by modern education in the mission schools, by the close connection of the Maronites with France, and by emigration to north and south America. Outside there lay country districts where sharecroppers worked for urban landowners, and the great cities of Muslim culture and of a political consciousness basically Muslim, but now coloured with the new ideas of Ottoman liberalism, pan-Islam and Arab nationalism, all of them embodying in one way or another the ideas of a large, independent, united state in which there would be no place for special autonomies under foreign protection.
> ('Lebanon: The Development of a Political Society', in Hourani, 1981: 135–6)

Hence, the different communities of Lebanon added one more item to their long list of differences. Each one had its own perception of the national interest, and its relationship to the outside world.

The order the European powers fashioned in the 1860s was brought to an end at the end of the First World War. Out of the wreckage of the war, the French mandatory authorities were to create Greater Lebanon. Hourani has never traced this subject as carefully as when writing about other important developments.[3]

The attitude among the different communities to the 1920 creation of Greater Lebanon is best summarized as the follow-

---

3. For examples of his passive reaction to the emergence of Greater Lebanon, see 'Lebanon: The Development of a Political Society', in Hourani, 1981: 136; and Hourani, 1986: 12. See also Salibi, 1965; Salibi, 1976; and Zamir, 1988.

ing. Greek Catholics and Maronites fully supported a separate Greater Lebanon; the Greek Orthodox were divided; and the Sunnis and most of the Shi'is strongly opposed it, as did many of the Druze. Hourani, however, gives us more insight into the thinking of these communities:

> Many Maronites still remained loyal in their hearts to the smaller Lebanon, and did not face the implications of the inclusion in it of Beirut and Tripoli. Most Sunni Muslims were loyal to the idea of an Arab nation and an Arab Syrian state, and were unwilling to accept the change from being part of the political community of the Ottoman Empire to being only one community among others; the Muslims of Tripoli feared that their trade would be strangled — Lebanon did not need two ports of the size of Beirut and Tripoli. Shi'i Muslims derived some benefit from the existence of Lebanon, since for the first time they were recognised legally as a separate community, but they too felt the pull of Arab nationalism. Many of the Orthodox Christians were unwilling to be part of a state where Maronites would dominate and France be always present: their political ideal was either 'Arab' or 'Syrian' (the idea of a secular united Syrian nation, popular among Christians of Beirut in the late nineteenth century, had been carried from there to the emigrant colonies, and was now brought back to Lebanon by the son of an emigrant, who made it the basis of a party which offered an alternative to Lebanese or Arab nationalism).
>
> ('Lebanon: The Development of a Political Society', in Hourani, 1981: 137)

Lebanon: The Pull of the Ancestors

The last part of this quotation is of great importance; indeed it is one of the few statements that reflect Hourani's personal view on a major issue about which he felt strongly. This point, therefore, deserves a closer look.

The son of the emigrant about whom he wrote was Antun Sa'ada, founder of the Syrian Social Nationalist Party in 1932. In 1949, Sa'ada and his followers attempted to overthrow the government in Lebanon. The plot failed, and Sa'ada was 'hastily tried and executed' (Hourani, 1962a: 317). Three types of contending nationalism were in the air of 1920s Lebanon: Arab, Syrian and Lebanese. The first two would lose to the third. Arab nationalism was a mere slogan (although troublesome for some time to come), and Syrian nationalism lost its attractiveness: 'As time passed and there grew up a new generation which accepted as natural frontiers which had been artificial, the idea of geographical [Greater] Syria lost its force' (Hourani, 1962a: 319). No doubt, Hourani was part of that new generation. It is fascinating to note that when Judge Joe Hutcheson of the 1946 Anglo-American Committee of Inquiry asked the 30-year-old Hourani if he was a Syrian, his answer was 'Yes' (Anglo-American Committee of Inquiry, 25 March 1946: 131).[4] In addition, other questions remain: What was it in Antun Sa'ada's frame of mind that captured the imagination of Hourani?

> By a detailed study of history [Sa'ada] tried to show that there was in this sense a Syrian nation, with a common

---

4. Copy provided by Hourani. During an interview with Hourani in London, 13 May 1991, he said he answered yes only because of the circumstances.

social consciousness developed over a long period of history. It included the inhabitants of the whole of geographical Syria, and had continued to exist as a separate entity even when incorporated in larger empires or broken up into smaller states. It had existed long before Islam; after the rise of Islam, its great days were those of the Umayyad caliphate, a Syrian State acting in conformity with the principles of Syrian civilization. Politically, Sa'ada stood for the reunion of this unit and its complete political independence. Internally, he advocated the creation of a genuine and deep social unity, and for this there were two conditions. The first was the complete separation of religion and politics. So long as this did not exist, internal division would continue; for 'religious-political considerations', the separate existence of Lebanon was temporarily necessary. The second condition was far-reaching social and economic reform.

(Hourani, 1962a: 318)

Hourani appeared to develop his thinking along the same lines as those of the Syrian Social National Party, first believing in an independent united Syrian nation, then, after 1945, in the justification for a Greater Syrian nation as a prerequisite for a united Arab nation. In short, Syrian nationalism, no longer capable of achieving its immediate goals, was submerged by Arab nationalism.

Writing in 1946, Hourani was to endorse political independence for Syria and Lebanon from French rule (Hourani, 1946b: 268). Independence would enable them to unify, a prerequisite for their becoming a part of a future Arab state. Later, in 1966, he regretted the timing of his judgement regarding their readiness for self-government. Hourani came to believe that the French departure from Lebanon was taken too soon. He observed that 'by the time the French left the communal system had scarcely been working long enough to become an unchallenged tradition' ('Lebanon: The Development of a Political Society', in Hourani, 1981: 137–8). France implanted in Lebanon a new communal arrangement, the newly born Greater Lebanon in place of the old *mutasarrifiyya*, an electoral system, and a chamber of deputies. The French, however, did not stay long enough for the Lebanese to master the craft of French liberalism and adapt to its practice. They stayed long enough to become a *de facto* guardian of the new social contract. France retreated in the early 1940s, setting aside her historical ties to the Maronites. Direct European rule was past. France had been unable to tutor the Lebanese in the arts of political liberalism, or bequeath them a viable sense of nationalism. France had given the communities of Lebanon some time: she left them with the accord that was to take them into the wave of independence: the National Pact of 1943.

The National Pact institutionalized the informal practices of the country: an unofficial agreement was reached whereby the Lebanese president would be a Maronite, the prime minister a Sunni, and the president of the chamber of deputies a Shi'i. Hourani perceived this accommodation to be the product of two factors. First, Arab nationalists saw post-Second World War France as an exhausted power and thought the moment ripe to rid itself of the mandate. Second, the merchant class thought it was in its best interest to do away with France, an action that would allow them to control the machinery of government and, thus, safeguard their interests and establish closer relations with other countries. On the surface, this looked like a decent arrangement but, in reality, it was not.

Instead, each holder of the top three leadership positions — the presidency of the state, the prime ministry, and the head of the chamber of deputies — only considered and reflected the interest of his own community.

> The 'National Pact' expressed the difference as well as the unity of the sects. All might speak of a Lebanese nation, and of equality between the sects, but they meant different things. For some, Lebanon was still essentially a Maronite national home; for some, a Christian refuge; for some, a secular state based on a scarcely existing national unity; for some a temporary expedient until a broad, secular Arab state should be ready to absorb it.
> ('Lebanon: The Development of a Political Society', in Hourani, 1981: 140–1)

According to Hourani, what the National Pact of 1943 was intended to do was harmonize and accommodate those who thought they were part of Christendom (mainly Maronites) and those (Muslims) whose loyalty belonged to the Arab world. It was an accommodation whereby the Sunnis would not push Arab nationalism and the Maronites would not push too restrictive a view of Lebanese nationalism. As early as 1957, Hourani made an accurate prediction of the durability of the National Pact:

> The National Pact has stood the test of time, in the sense that Lebanon still exists, and that most Lebanese accept it. But the Pact was made not so much to express a unity as to reconcile differences, and each side accepted it not out of enthusiastic conviction but rather because there was nothing else to be done. It is natural therefore that

the link it established between differing points of view
should sometimes be in danger of breaking.

(Hourani, 1957b: 137)

Indeed, it broke in 1958 when the differences between those
who looked to the West and those who looked to the East
came to the surface and had to be reconciled. The civil war of
1958 was caused mainly by internal rivalries and by the
disagreements among neutralist Arab nationalism, symbolized
by Jamal 'Abd al-Nasir, and the 'West', led by the United States.
There were some months of civil turmoil, but the leaders of the
different divisions in Lebanon were eventually able to come
together and form a government. The fragility and artificial
nature of the National Pact is one of the major themes in
Hourani's analyses of Lebanese history.

Is it conceivable to assume that until recently the history of
post–1920 Lebanon has been the step-by-step enlargement of
the political heritage of the Christian parts of the mountainside
and the gradual introduction of the Druzes, Shi'is, and Sunnis
into a political conception that had came into existence among
the Maronites? This was the view of the Lebanonists, and it
was a view with which Hourani took issue. His judgement on
this question can be seen in his critical appraisal of Kamal
Salibi's *Modern History of Lebanon*. Salibi had given the
'Lebanonists' position' its most sustained and compelling case.
In Hourani's critique could be discerned a broader view that
went beyond Mount Lebanon.

> Dr Salibi's account of events is, as always, clear and fair,
> but it may be that he misses a dimension of it. While
> understanding that the idea of 'Christian Lebanon' was
> no longer valid after 1920, he perhaps tends to see the

Muslims as non-Lebanese who had to be turned into Lebanese, rather than as people who had something positive to contribute to the process. It is almost unavoidable that someone writing the history of Lebanon should view it as that of the expansion of a mountain community: the princes of south Lebanon extending their rule over the north, the Maronites from the north moving into the south, the north and south united in a single entity absorbing the sea-coast. This may be a correct picture until 1920, but after that the nature of the process changes: the political culture of the mountain-valleys meets the quite different political culture of the coastal cities. The Sunni population of Tripoli, Beirut and Sayda was heir to the political culture of the Ottoman Empire; if it was to enter the Lebanese community, it could only do so by bringing its inheritance with it, and this included a different aptitude not only toward the relationship of Lebanon with the outside world but also towards the relationship of spiritual and temporal, of government and society, of leaders and masses.

('Lebanon from Feudalism to Nation State', in Hourani, 1981: 147)

Salibi wasted no time in taking advantage of this criticism. In fact, the main theme of his 1988 work, *A House of Many Mansions: The History of Lebanon Reconsidered*, is in large part influenced by Hourani's vision of how the historian should re-examine Lebanese history. Salibi writes:

Here we have another image of Ottoman Lebanon: not the mountain alone — whose political history, in its

basic pattern, had close parallels in many different corners of the Arab world between the sixteenth century and the nineteenth; but the marriage of the mountain with Beirut, both partners interacting, stage by stage, with influences from the West arriving through a variety of channels. In this marriage, the tribal mountain, with its feudal organization under the Maans and the Shihabs, could sometimes wield political control over Beirut. On the other hand, more discreet influences radiating from Beirut came with time to permeate the mountains — an aspect of the history of Lebanon which was *first* brought to notice and emphasized in the work of Albert Hourani.
(Salibi, 1981: 163, my emphasis)

The tension between 'city' and 'mountain' — really a debate between the country's 'Lebanonist' mission and her Arab calling — inspired Hourani to write what many experts on Lebanon regard as the most powerful essay on the subject: 'Ideologies of the Mountain and City' (in Hourani, 1981: 170–8).[5] In it Hourani explored the nature of the ambivalence and mistrust between city dwellers and communities of the mountain. This, however, was only a starting point for Hourani, who added his own creativity and originality to his analyses. Another inspiration for his writing this essay was his reading of *Mediterranean Countrymen: Essays in the Social Anthropology of the Mediterranean* (Pitt-Rivers, 1963),[6] a book of essays by a group of anthropologists. The main interest of this group was the differing effects on Mediterranean societies of the predominant religion (whether Catholicism, Eastern Orthodoxy,

---

5. Interview with Hourani, Washington, DC, 11 May 1989.
6. On the importance of this work to him, see Hourani, 1981: 232.

or Islam). Among these anthropologists, Hourani was most influenced by J. C. Baroja, a Spanish anthropologist whose main thesis was proving the inefficacy of studying the countryside without also studying its relationship to the city.

Thus far, the history of Lebanon has not been the gradual expansion of the Maronite part of the mountain and the slow transformation of other political beliefs to fit the ideology of the former. The political leadership of Lebanon, the *zu'ama*, involves three types, or modes, of political activity:

> First, there is the 'feudal' mode: that of the great lords of those parts of the countryside where large estates and traditional lordships exist (among Druzes and Shi'is in the south, Shi'is in the Biqa', and Sunnis in 'Akkar). Their power rests on their position as landowners, often of ancient lineage, their use of strong-arm men, and their ability to give protection and patronage. Secondly, there are the 'populist' politicians of the mainly Christian regions in the northern half of the country, where smallholdings are common, and leadership has less of a solid base of socio-economic power, and is derived on the one hand from the use of powers of protection and patronage to maintain political 'clans', on the other from some kind of ideology or programme of action. Thirdly, there are the leaders of the Muslim populations of the coastal cities; they also obtain and retain leadership by ideological appeal and the exercise of patronage, but add to these a third source of power, the manipulation of the urban masses, mobilised for them by the 'strong-arm' men of the popular quarters, the *qabaday's*.
>
> ('Ideologies of the Mountain and the City' (1976), reprinted in Hourani, 1981: 172–3)

Whatever their devotion or primeval loyalties, all three types of leadership had to use certain ideological appeals to maintain control in their communities.

There were two types of ideologies dominating the political climate of Lebanon: the ideology of the mountain and the ideology of the city. The ideology of the mountain was peculiar to the Maronite community. Other communities on the mountain had attained considerable solidarity but never enough to enable them to produce political ideas that could constitute a course of action. The ideological development of the Maronite community can be divided into three aspects, each with a sequential connection to a different period of their history. The first aspect is the notion of Lebanon as a 'compact community' whereby the Maronites live among themselves under the rule of their churches, and protect themselves against the assault of Muslims of the coast and plains.

> Maronites are aware of themselves as the only Catholic 'nation' in the Middle East, and indeed of Asia, and are therefore sensitive to any doubts cast on their Catholicism; the idea of the 'perpetual orthodoxy' of the Maronite, and Leo X's description of them as 'a rose among thorns', have been themes of Maronite writers.
> ('Ideologies of the Mountain and the City' (1976), reprinted in Hourani, 1981: 173)

The second aspect is the idea of Lebanon existing within a political framework controlled by the political elite of the prominent Sunni, Druze and Maronite families. This idea is based upon the role of the seventeenth-century Druze prince Fakhr al-Din II, the founder of both the principle of communal alliance and Lebanese sovereignty. Finally, there is the concept of 'populism', a different appeal made by a new kind of contender for leadership. It was the populist leaders who in the 1860s led the insurrection of smallholders in Kisrawan against the Khazin family and organized the popular movement by the growing Christian market towns of Zahla and Dayr al-Qamar against the traditional Druze leadership of the towns. In one way or another, the later Phalanges were the inheritors of this tradition of populism ('Ideologies of the Mountain and the City' (1976), reprinted in Hourani, 1981: 174–5).

Populism took hold in the Christian villages of the north much more easily than it did throughout the south. The northern part of Mount Lebanon did not have a highly developed feudal structure; it was always under more direct rule by the Mamluks and later by the Ottomans. Distrust and suspicion of the cities and its peoples were the main attributes of mountain populism. 'For the villager, rural society is created by God, urban by man; the life of the field is 'natural' life and in all its purity' ('Ideologies of the Mountain and the City' (1976), reprinted in Hourani, 1981: 175). It should be kept in mind that the Lebanon of the eighteenth and nineteenth centuries did not include the larger towns of the coast. Nevertheless, in 1920 with the creation of 'Greater Lebanon', the city of Beirut became a great centre of commercial activity and communications. The city of Beirut 'became not only a part but the dominant part of the country, and from it there came other *ideas* of what Lebanon was or should be' ('Ideologies of the Mountain and the City' (1976), reprinted in Hourani, 1981, my emphasis).

Important here for Hourani was that the urban idea of Lebanon was neither of a society closed against the outside world, nor of a unitary society in which smaller communities were dissolved, but something between the two. It was a plural society in which communities, still different on the level of inherited religious loyalties and intimate family ties, coexisted within a common framework ('Ideologies of the Mountain and the City' (1976), reprinted in Hourani, 1981: 175).

It is fair enough to say that other states in the Arab world had been put together by colonial rule. Yet Lebanon's dilemma was unique. The country had a 'soft' state, incapable of upholding a viable social contract, and a number of cabinets that were too weak for a state living in a rough neighbourhood.

From the 1920s onward, the ideology of the city conquered but never killed the ideology of the mountain. It dominated the material component of the mountain but never the spiritual one. 'The new immigrants into the cities seemed to be more conscious of sectarian differences than those living in the countryside' ('Ideologies of the Mountain and the City' (1976), reprinted in Hourani, 1981: 177). Beirut, in this sense is 'a microcosm of Lebanon's fragmented political culture' (Khalaf, 1987: 265). With the civil troubles of 1860 and the emergence of the 'commercial cities', the mountain communities were no longer able to stay in seclusion. To the city of Beirut, the new immigrants brought their anxieties, their mountain populism, and their suspicion of the other communities. In Hourani's view, the civil war of 1975 proved how brittle the social basis was. Emphasis had been placed on the institution of the presidency, the thinking being that it could rise above clan and sectarian differences. There had been an accord between Sunni and Maronite politicians, but it had failed to bring their communities together. In this regard, the Lebanese scholar Fouad Ajami wrote: 'The City's great myth — that it was a place where Islam and Christianity met and fashioned a society of compromise — had collapsed' (Reed and Ajami, 1988: 10). Hourani's story of the mountain republic that transformed itself into the city-state will remain a work of great and seminal importance.⁷

Hourani's work takes us from the earlier troubles of the country to the remaking of the political order in 1975. Into the new disordered landscape, however, he was reluctant to venture. He offers the consoling thought that the turmoil of later years may have driven home the point that no one wants Lebanon to be destroyed and the reality of the 'being' of Lebanon as a nation-state cannot and will not be debated (interview with Hourani, London, 11 May 1991). He had little faith in the institution of the presidency, partially because Lebanon is a small country where everybody knows everybody else. According to Hourani, the president felt pressure all the time — from his family, from the church, and the local 'bosses' or *zu'ama*. They always came to him with endless demands, and he spent all of his time and energy dealing with little affairs. One president, however, met the approval of Hourani's image of an effective leader for a country like Lebanon.

> General Fu'ad Shihab was a soldier and not a politician. He was not part of Beirut's political and commercial society, and rather despised it. Following de Gaulle, he might have said that he had a certain idea of Lebanon. He tried to create a strong executive and move the Lebanese economy in new directions, but beyond certain

---

7. It has been fashionable among those who are concerned about Lebanon to give all the credit for Hourani's innovative ideas to the 'Ideologies of the Mountain and the City' (1976). Equal credit must, however, be given to his 1966 essay, 'Lebanon: The Development of a Political Society'. Both are reprinted in Hourani, 1981.

limits he had no lasting success; he had no effective
political support or adequate structure of administration
(Hourani, 1986: 14)

On the other hand, most Lebanese politicians were small-time
politicians who had no real feel for statesmanship, or statecraft,
which comes when a leader takes responsibility for a large
country.

A small, weak country, lying in an important position,
cannot prevent its internal conflicts becoming the
channels through which great powers win influence and
pursue their rivalries.
(Hourani, 1981: 141)

The breakdown in the civil society of Lebanon had internal
causes that were taken advantage of by external forces such as
Israel, Syria and later Iran. Although Hourani's narratives on
the subject go up to the 1975 civil war, he does not take
account of the post–1967 Palestinian presence in Lebanon and
its influence on the political life of the country. The Palestinians represented their own distinct community, among
others, which used and was used by others to fulfill different
political agendas.

Over half a century ago, in his major treatise on Syria and
Lebanon, Hourani wrote of his own concept of what Lebanon
ought to be:

On one hand, it should have a relation with Syria and
the other Arab countries which is much more than the
external relation of independent States to one another;
on the other, it should have liberty to develop its own

life and make its own choices. It should possess a character of its own as a centre of Christian life, of Western culture and of religious toleration; but its life should be for the whole of the Arab world and not for itself alone.

(Hourani, 1946b: 265)

Lebanon's history must have been a terrible disappointment. We must not forget that at the time Hourani wrote this, Arab nationalism was alive and well; it was still possible to think that the fragments of which Lebanon consisted could be homogenized. This was a limited vision of Lebanon, but, nonetheless, violence was to overtake this vision. It was before the troubles of 1975 that Hourani wrote about the 'first republic' that the Lebanese had put together. Whether the 'second republic' will fare better remains to be seen. History could repeat itself.

6

Conclusion: The Legacy of an Intellectual Mediator

The index of Albert Hourani's major work of synthesis, *A History of the Arab Peoples* has eight references to the work of the great Muslim philosopher Ibn Sina (Avicenna, 980–1037) and one reference to Yasir Arafat of the Palestine Liberation Organization. It has ten references to the life and work of the incomparable North African historian and sociologist Ibn Khaldun (1332–1406) and a single, solitary reference to Saddam Hussein, the ruler of Iraq. The jurist Ahmad Ibn Hanbal (780–855) gets seven references while the Syrian ruler Hafiz al-Asad gets only three passing references. The list could be expanded.

It is with broad civilizational analysis that Albert Hourani felt at home, with the general sweep of Arab history. The twists and turns of Arab politics, the military coups and the intermittent rebellions held very little interest for him. He was a historian of ideas and mentalities and culture. In a critical review in the *Wall Street Journal*, the American political historian Daniel Pipes dismisses *A History of the Arab Peoples* as an apologetic work, both on old historical matters and modern problems of Arab politics. Pipes observes that Hourani drew an 'overly rosy' picture of the Arab past and present.

When it comes to the modern era, Mr. Hourani is even more apologetic. He characterizes the period since 1967, for instance, as 'a disturbance of the spirits' — overlooking the traumas and acute crises of the past quarter century. Arab regimes regularly lost wars, squandered oil revenues and brutalized their own populations. Whether the statistics concern health, literacy, or indoor plumbing, the record is poor, and matters are dismal when it comes to artistic or religious expression.

(Pipes, 1991: 18)

Daniel Pipes's attack misses the entire thrust of Hourani's work. Pipes tips his hand when he adds that Hourani 'pursues a fashionably leftist agenda, impugning capitalism and attacking Israel' (Pipes, 1991: 18). There has never been a trace of leftist-Marxist analysis in Hourani's work. Everything Hourani wrote was anchored in a classical liberal outlook — a belief in pluralism, distrust of grand causes and of single explanations of history and society. He had an aversion to radical violence and forced social change. True enough, he did not dwell on this or that revolt or deed of repression. He was after the social and cultural forces that made for the continuity of a civilization, and for the persistence of a dominant intellectual and political tradition that saw the Arab world through centuries of turbulence and change. Pipes is keen to look at the instances when the order broke down. Throughout his long scholarly career Hourani sought to study the institutions, the traditions, the intellectual luminaries and philosophers and schools of thought that gave Arab society coherence and resilience.

The best illustration of Hourani's method and goal as a

Conclusion: The Legacy of an Intellectual Mediator

scholar — and a sure rebuttal to the charge levelled against him by Pipes and others who did not find in Hourani's work what they were looking for — is the four-page prologue to *A History of the Arab Peoples*. He chooses for his subject the life and career of the fourteenth century philosopher Ibn Khaldun. He follows the journey of Ibn Khaldun from his birth in Tunis into a family that hailed from southern Arabia, to his religious education, his service to the ruler of Tunis, his passage to Granada, capital of the last surviving kingdom of Muslim Spain, where he gained and then lost the ruler's favour, and his subsequent departure to Cairo in his fiftieth year, where he was to remain until his death. Ibn Khaldun knew favour and banishment; his family perished when they all drowned on a sea voyage from Tunis to Alexandria. Everything around him seemed to be in flux. But there were things that never gave way. This is Hourani's summation of the cultural forces that endured and sustained Ibn Khaldun's world and that of his contemporaries and other Muslims and Arabs after him, through all kinds of upheaval.

> Something was stable, however, or seemed to be. A world where a family from southern Arabia could move to Spain, and after six centuries return nearer to its place of origin and still find itself in familiar surroundings, had a unity which transcended divisions of time and space; the Arabic language could open the door to office and influence throughout that world; a body of knowledge, transmitted over the centuries by a known chain of teachers, preserved a moral community even when rulers changed; places of pilgrimage, Mecca and Jerusalem, were unchanging poles of the human world even if power shifted from one city to another; and belief in a

God who created and sustained the world could give meaning to the blows of fate.

(Hourani, 1991a: 4)

Until the intrusion of the West, this balance continued to work. This consisted of the process that held Hourani's attention after he left policy analysis and the work of the Foreign Office and the plunge he took into the struggle for Palestine. Martin Kramer, another critic of Hourani, gets closer to the truth than Pipes when he says that to write the history he did, Hourani had to slight politics and that he did so by averting his eyes 'from politics, from state society' (Kramer, 1991: 56). This is a shrewd observation, which comes close to the heart of Hourani's enterprise. Of Hourani's method, Kramer adds (with a critical tone):

> Hourani steers his narrative out of the palace gates and into busy urban quarters, villages and tribal encampments. We are escorted through markets and workshops, we measure the width of the streets. We enter the courtyards of mosques and homes, we pause to admire the gardens and furnishings. We see the pilgrims off to Mecca, and when plague strikes, we number the dead. At several points, the narrative soars upward, to survey the lay of the land, the soil, the weather.
>
> (Kramer, 1991: 56)

Kramer intends this passage as an illustration of the theme that Hourani studies, and then the things he omits. He faults him for overlooking 'the violence that has been close to the surface of the Arab experience at all times, not only in politics and war, but in the regulated conduct of social and economic life' (Kramer, 1991: 56). He further observes: 'Nor does Hourani open a way to comprehend the shuddering violence that has descended upon the Arabs in the 1990s, although his book will be read most widely for just that purpose' (Kramer, 1991: 57). By the violence of the 1990s, Kramer is most likely speaking of the violence of the Gulf War of 1990/1. If so, his analysis is correct, but perhaps beside the point. Hourani never claimed for himself that political territory. While it is true that this son of Arab immigrants to Britain preferred to see the bright or durable side of Arab political culture, he was no apologist for the excesses of Arab politics. He was disillusioned by the failures of Arab politics, by the breakdown of what pluralism it possessed. Anyone who misses that dimension of his work has not read it with care.

It was a matter of style that Hourani did not emphasize what was cruel or oppressive. His sensibility was that of a scholar who searched for order in human affairs, for consensus, for the common ground on which political men met. This was so when he wrote of Arab politics or of Western policies for that matter. He was never shrill or dogmatic. His scholarly and personal demeanor precluded a frontal assault on his subject matter. He did not think that pointing out the particularly unattractive features of Arab politics was what a scholarly vocation should consist of. In both his writings and his long career as a teacher, he taught the importance of patience when examining societies. He conceived of history in large periods. He did not think a scholar could understand a people, a society, or a political culture by aiming a strong, intrusive light on them when their ways were under stress. He was uncomfortable with simple or monistic explanations of political phenomena. The noted Oxford economic historian Roger Owen — a student, then a colleague of Hourani — described his method at the Requiem Mass held for Hourani at St Aloysius Church in Oxford on 25 January 1993, as one of 'progressive revelation'. Hourani's approach, said Owen in his eulogy of the scholar, was 'to concentrate on the peoples of the Middle East, on their communities, and most of all on their cities, on their intricate relations of power and influence mediated by a vibrant, often stormy, but always exciting current of ideas' (Owen, 1993: 1).[1]

Complexity marked the Houranian world described by Roger Owen:

> This was a world of large commercial cities like his native Manchester and his adopted Beirut with their busy exchange, their traffic in ideas and their refusal to be penned in by geography and tradition. For him the life of such cities was at its most resonant in the 'Liberal Age', the era exemplified by the resolute certainties of Mr Gladstone to whom his father had gone to listen to on his first Sunday in England in 1891. In the same spirit Albert welcomed Arab independence, but then became increasingly uncomfortable as its early pluralism began to give way to an illiberal authoritarianism.
>
> (Owen, 1993: 3)

Owen takes us close to the heart of Hourani's intellectual vocation. Hourani was interested in ideas, but he saw ideas, as another former student and colleague of his, Derek Hopwood

---

1. The Centre for Lebanese Studies, Oxford, England, kindly made available to this author proofs of a collection of eulogies on Albert Hourani by his former colleagues.

Conclusion: The Legacy of an Intellectual Mediator

remarked, as 'delicate and complex as butterflies' (Centre for Lebanese Studies, 1993: 13). He was interested in the elaboration of public order, and he saw order as the subtle work of generations bequeathing to their successors their knowledge, their intellectual style and their living tradition. All this required a great amount of historical patience. And it was incumbent on the scholar to tread carefully, to refrain from judging societies too harshly. The key to this method, Hopwood is right to remind us, may be found, most fittingly, in a foreword Hourani wrote to the French Orientalist Jacques Berque's book, *Imperialism and Revolution*:

> Is it possible to grasp the essential nature of a country other than one's own? Yes, in the sense in which one can know a human being other than oneself: through patience, clarity and love and with a final acceptance of the mystery of otherness.
> (Centre for Lebanese Studies, 1993: 15, remarks of Derek Hopwood)

For Hourani the Arab world was something between 'otherness' and one's own country. (The same is no doubt true of England.) He savored the intricacies of Arab politics and left as rich a body of writing as has been attempted in this century. His principal themes will endure. And it is fitting in a concluding assessment to recapitulate these themes.

First, Hourani understood the urban basis of political order, the place of the 'Islamic city' in the creation and maintenance of public order. It is no exaggeration to say that his inquiries into Arab history are inquiries into the life of its dominant cities. He depicted the 'two poles' of the city — the palace and the market, and was forever intrigued by the terms of the relationship between the ruler and the marketplace. He knew that such links were precarious and shifting, 'moving on a spectrum between alliance and hostility' (Hourani, 1991a: 135). The public order of the city could not be taken for granted: the ruler, the 'notables', and the *'ulama* were the pillars of the urban order; cities thrived when the alliance of interests worked; they failed, or succumbed to the urban mob, when this alliance came apart.

Hourani had not started out as a student of the cities of Islam. He had had his beginning as a student of ideas. But once his interest was engaged he was to remain a curious student of urban politics — of the culture and style of cities. He was aware of the power of the urban crowd without showing that much interest in the stability of urban order. He did not exaggerate the power of the ruler. In one of his essays he elaborated on the social structure of the Islamic city, noting the connection between the 'commercial bourgeoisie' and the *'ulama*. Such ties, such resources as the *'ulama* and the merchants possessed, were a check on the power of the ruler.

> Members of the great bourgeois families and of the *'ulama* together provided an urban leadership: their wealth, piety, culture, and ancient names gave them social prestige, and the patronage of quarters, ethnic or religious groups, crafts or the city as a whole.
> ('The Islamic City', in Hourani, 1981: 28)

No single model of a despotic authority would capture the complexity of this urban culture. Its peace was held together not mainly by the ruler's whip but by the formal institutions and the informal arrangements worked out by its constituent groups. The peace of the Islamic city held for long stretches of time, Hourani tells us. It broke down during an interregnum when a dynasty or a state had collapsed or been defeated in war. Even then the turmoil was short-lived: the local leaders, the 'notables' would step forth as a provisional government: 'they would administer the city for a time, until one of them emerged as ruler, or until they had to hand it over to its new master' ('The Islamic City', in Hourani, 1981: 30).

Hourani insisted on the peculiarly 'Islamic' roots of the urban culture of the Arab world. Cities were not unique to Islam, of course. The features of urban life were transcultural. There was still, though, something distinctive about the role Islamic law and institutions played in the life of Islamic cities:

> To say that 'Islamic civilisation was urban' may be commonplace but is still valid to some extent. The Islamic institutions were concentrated in the cities: mosques, schools, *zawiyas*. They possessed a kind of prestige and strength which neither rulers nor bourgeoisie could ignore, and it was for this reason that they provided a framework for urban life. Through them the ruler's acts should be legitimised, the city-dwellers could take corporate action, and the two could be morally linked, the close connection of the *'ulama* with the bourgeoisie gave a distinctive shape to the urban society of the Islamic world.
> ('The Islamic City', in Hourani, 1981: 34)

A second and related recurring theme in his work is the power and the role of the 'notables' — the 'natural' leaders of the town dwellers, or what Max Weber, called the 'patriciate'. This bequest will remain as one of Hourani's great themes. Two generations of his students have returned to this theme time and again. Notables and their ways fascinated Hourani. He saw the power of the notables as the cornerstone of the old order in the Arab world, until it was undone by the age of mass-based nationalism.

As Hourani describes it, patrician politics, or politics of notables arises when specific conditions are met:

- When society is ordered by relations of personal dependence: that is, the artisan produces for the patrician patrons; the peasant in the countryside is dependent on the landowner in the city.
- When society is dominated by urban notables, great families who reside in the city.
- When the notables have some freedom of political action vis-à-vis the ruler.

The principal pillars of the politics of notables are access to authority, and a social power that the notables possess on their own. It is this kind of politics that anchored the old order, under Ottoman rule, for four centuries. In the Ottoman age, imperial power was remote; it needed intermediaries. This is where the notables came in. They were beneficiaries of the Ottoman method of control, for the Ottomans tried 'not to crush and absorb but to preserve or even revive good local customs ('Ottoman Reform and the Politics of Notables', in Hourani, 1981: 44).

The notables of the Houranian world were drawn from a multitude of endeavours. First, there were the *'ulama*, the religious notables, with their primacy in the spheres of law, education and ideology. Second, there were the leaders of the local garrisons. Third, there were the 'secular notables' — individuals or families whose power rested on the possession

Conclusion: The Legacy of an Intellectual Mediator 163

of a political or military tradition, or the control of agricultural production.

Centralization and modernization were of course anathema to the notables. The more the Ottoman modernizers sought to knit together their large state, the greater the threat to the autonomy of the notables. The balance was never even between the imperial centre in Istanbul and the Arab notables. In North Africa the local order of power was strongest — so great the distance from Istanbul, so weak the power of the Ottoman navy. There was more even balance in Cairo because Egypt, Hourani reminds us, was too important to be left alone.

There would be serious consequences for this politics of notables when the age of imperialism descended on the Arabs. These notables, pre-eminent in local affairs, had no knowledge of international politics. Sheltered and buffered by Ottoman authorities, the notables had no exposure to the harsh realities of statecraft. Their horizons were limited. Istanbul had spared them the need to learn the ways of states. It is obvious from Hourani's work — though he himself did not directly say it, that such classes of men, such families, were in no position to take on the power of the West, or to comprehend what threat its power meant. The Ottoman age, an age of notables, had not prepared the Arabs for the trauma of independence. The notables were prepared to defend their small prerogatives. They knew how to appeal to Istanbul or to avoid its circulars. They had little if any knowledge of what states do. This had been Istanbul's monopoly. Hourani's work gives us a definitive account of the workings of this world of notables. His landmark essay 'Ottoman Reform and the Politics of Notables' depicts the notables' attempt to delay Ottoman centralization in the 1850s, and their ultimate failure. The notables could postpone the moment of reckoning. Riding anti-European and anti-Christian feelings the notables would give themselves, in the mid-nineteenth century, some room for manoeuvre. Fighting against the foreign consulates and the foreign merchants, as they did in Aleppo in 1850, Mosul in 1854, Nablus in 1856, and Damascus in 1860, the notables expressed 'traditional' society's anguish and demoralization. But before these forces, and then in the face of popular nationalism, the world of the notables would eventually come apart.

A third theme of Albert Hourani's relates to the Ottoman background of the modern Arab world. Arab nationalism had accentuated the distance between the Arab world and its four Turkish centuries. The Christian intellectuals and writers, in particular, had been keen to separate the Arab world from its Ottoman past. But these Ottoman centuries, from the 1500s when many of the Arab provinces fell to the Turks until the collapse of the Ottoman Empire in the First World War, the Ottoman world had been home to the Arabs. Hourani's work makes the appropriate historical connection between the Arab present and the Ottoman past.

The foreign sympathizers of Arab nationalism, men such as T. E. Lawrence, had insisted on the 'darkness' of Ottoman rule, on the ruin that Ottoman rule brought to the Arabs. This is the caricature that Lawrence drew of the Ottoman centuries — and it is a caricature that was picked up by Arab nationalist historians. The Arabs, Lawrence wrote, had been free, the 'Semitic mind' untroubled, until the Turks came:

> With the coming of the Turks this happiness became a dream. By stages the Semites of Asia passed under their yoke, and found it a slow death. Their goods were stripped from them; and their spirits shrivelled in the numbing breath of a military Government. Turkish rule

was gendarme rule, and Turkish political theory as crude as its practice. The Turks taught the Arabs that the interests of a sect were higher than those of patriotism: that the petty concerns of the province were more than nationality. They led them by subtle dissensions to distrust one another.

(Lawrence, 1962: 42)

Hourani breaks with this interpretation of what Ottoman rule had been like. He emphasizes the continuity between Ottoman and Arab politics. Ottoman history was what the Arabs knew. The habits the empire transmitted — the attitude towards authority, the nature of political obligations, the very nature of what politics itself was made of — had been deeply influenced by the Ottoman tradition. Even the very social classes that had led the Arab nationalist movement, Hourani reminds us, had been Ottomanists to begin with. They had been shaped by their experiences in the Ottoman armies and secret societies. No political upheaval could shatter the bonds that had bound the Arabs with the Ottoman imperial past. Because Hourani's work became overwhelmingly preoccupied with social history, he could see the continuities that political historians were prone to miss. The guilds, the connection between religious and political life, the social order of the city, all of these bore the imprint of the Ottoman tradition. Here, too, it should be noted that Hourani had not started out with this outlook. His influential book *Arabic Thought in the Liberal Age* had accepted the idea of the Arab nationalists that their world was radically different from the Ottoman tradition. He shifted ground later as his interest in social and economic history evolved. The political revolutions had not changed the cultural traditions that had been elaborated over four long centuries. Hourani's work rehabilitates the Ottoman past, without ignoring its failures and shortcomings. There is in his work an understanding of the role the imperial centre in Istanbul had played in fending off the power of the West right up until the time the empire itself fell on hard times.

Fourthly, Hourani's name will long be associated with his analysis of, and contribution to, the study of Arab nationalism. Second perhaps only to George Antonius in the English-speaking world, Hourani stands out as an influential chronicler of Arab nationalism. In the case of Antonius, *The Arab Awakening* (1938, reprinted 1969) was a work of advocacy, plain and simple. The task was straightforward: Antonius wrote as a petitioner on behalf of Arab nationalism. He chronicled what he took to be the French and British betrayals of the promises they had made to the Arabs in the aftermath of the First World War. And of equal importance Antonius wrote as a defender of the Hashemite family and its right to the Arab territories of Syria, Iraq, Transjordan, Palestine, and Lebanon. Hourani's task was a more scholarly one, though one interspersed with some advocacy and sympathy.

It is to Hourani that we will owe our appreciation of the balance between the two roles played in the making of modern Arab nationalism: that of the Christian secularists, and that of the Muslim modernists. It is his pioneering work that gives us the most judicious assessment of these two forces.

We owe to Hourani as well an appreciation of the liberal roots of Arab nationalism or the liberal intention. Arab nationalism did take an illiberal direction, but the early impulse was liberal through and through. Hourani understood that the power of the West had imposed on Arab society the necessity of a nationalist response. He would never slight Arab nationalism or dismiss its legitimacy, because he was fully

Conclusion: The Legacy of an Intellectual Mediator

aware of the intrusive power of Europe. Nor would he join other historians when they took the excesses of Arab nationalism as proof that nationalism had been an utter failure, and that the Arabs would have been better off without it. To understand Hourani's intellectual approach to nationalism we need only compare him with his noted contemporary and rival, the late historian Elie Kedourie. Like Hourani, Kedourie was a man of two cultures — the Middle East and England. But unlike Hourani, Kedourie saw modern Arab nationalism as a malignant force in Arab life. Kedourie did not explain how these fragile societies were to make their way through a world of states. But he portrayed Arab nationalism and the 'new men' who led it as unleashing chaos and disorder on the Arabs. Kedourie saw the instability of Arab politics as a product of nationalism, and of the men who led it:

> This instability is increased by the character of the men who now compete for power. They are new men whose earliest and deepest political impulse is contempt for the ways of their fathers. Youth, which in most countries and ages has been a disqualification for the practice of government, has become, since the days of the Young Turks, an advantage in the contest for power. The dislocation of society is made more acute by estrangement between the generations. The young are those who possess the techniques of Europe which Middle Eastern society — so they insist — must adopt or perish. Therefore they know better than their fathers, and they have the key to political salvation. The passion and presumption of youth, their rooted belief in their ancestors' ignorance and folly, their inexperience and clumsiness in the exercise of power combine to deprive

them of that decorum and *gravitas* which impressed foreign observers in the Muslim ruling classes of past centuries, and which served to put a decent check on the full expression of greed and cruelty. Heaven knows that sedition, treason and civil war are common enough in Middle Eastern history, but only in the present age is revolution glorified as a necessary part of the political process, violence proclaimed beneficent and treason holy.

(Kedourie, 1984: 10)

Hourani's temperament inclined to a different reading of history. These 'new men' he saw as disadvantaged players in the game of nations. He may have despaired of the excesses of authoritarian nationalism, its impatience with civil liberties and dissent, its ineptness when it played the game of nations, but he would not dismiss it with the kind of finality and aversion that Elie Kedourie did. His sympathy for the Arab situation in the world — weakness abroad, military and political weakness in the face of Israel — would not permit him to write off nationalism as a force for ill.

A fifth theme is that passion of youth — the question of Palestine. Though he wrote of it little after the 1940s, his intellectual output will endure. Though an advocate, he understood the weakness of the Palestinians. He never blustered; he argued his case and that of the Palestinians with care. He knew the balance of forces, and knew that the Palestinian notables and the leaderless peasantry of Palestine were no match for the modern Zionist movement. But he was no less of a visionary when it came to his analysis of Israel's dilemma. The Israelis would prevail, he had warned, but the Palestinian problem could not be wished away. The following remark, written after the Six-Day War of 1967 illustrates his ability to get to the heart of the matter. Israel, he wrote would be tempted to do nothing about the Palestinians. But in time, he added, 'the Palestinian Arab nation may rise once more to haunt Israel, this time inside as well as outside its frontiers' (Hourani and Talmon, 1967: 15).

From the very beginning of the struggle between the Palestinians and the Zionists Hourani knew that this issue would come to poison Arab political life. He knew that it would serve as a great barrier between the Arabs and the West, that the military dictators and the demagogues would use it to discredit the fragile liberalism they opposed. Any serious look at what has happened in the Arab world since 1948 would bear witness to Hourani's clear vision and insight. So, too, would what Israel has had to confront in its dealings with the Palestinians. The Israelis could never assimilate the Palestinians because they wanted a Jewish state. They could never repress the Palestinians into submission, so in the end, a quarter-century after they occupied the West Bank and Gaza, the Israelis had to search for an accommodation with the Palestinians.

To his concern for Palestine's Arabs, Hourani brought a liberal historian's belief in justice and self-determination. At the heart of his concern lay a straightforward belief in the 'justice of the nations'. His faith in England had been particularly strong: Pax Britannica, he was sure, would deliver justice. The balance of force, he knew, was tipped against the Palestinians. But he knew better than to believe that force alone would define order and make it stick. Any intellectual encounter with the history of the Israeli-Palestinian conflict would be incomplete without a reading of Hourani's briefs and essays. He was free of venom toward the Jewish enterprise in Palestine. He sought to achieve a reconciliation between the power of the Zionists and the national rights of the Palestinians.

A sixth major contribution of Hourani's lies in his study of his ancestral land: the political society of Lebanon. In its own way Lebanon is a microcosm for the ethnically fragmented states of the Middle East. Unique as it is, with its Druze, Maronites, Shi'is, Sunnis and other communities, Lebanon speaks to a broader Middle Eastern dilemma — the uneasy mix of national boundaries and ethnic communities. Thus, in his treatment of Lebanon, Hourani has helped us understand the political dilemmas of multi-sectarian societies — the conditions under which they thrive and the conditions under which they come apart.

Hourani presents a rich and poignant view of Lebanon, tinged with affection for the country. He knew the power of geography, the tension between mountain and city, the attitude of the people of the mountain toward the political doctrines of the city (Arab nationalism). He provided a key to understanding the fragmented political culture of the Fertile Crescent. Powerful states rule over the populations of Iraq and Syria, so the blood letting that became Lebanon's lot was not to be found in either of those two countries, for example. But a close look at the tension between centre and periphery in Lebanon, at the different world of the ethnic and religious communities can be revealing of the crisis of national integration in various Arab societies. (Other societies the world over, multiethnic societies everywhere, can be studied the same way, but it is the Arab world that concerns us here.)

A final central theme of Hourani's scholarship, one that runs through all his work and that runs through this study of his life and intellectual legacy is of course the political and intellectual relationship between the West and the world of the

Conclusion: The Legacy of an Intellectual Mediator

Arabs and Islam. The force of what Hourani gave us there derives, as repeatedly stated, from the facts of his life and biography. He belonged to the two worlds, and he spent a lifetime trying to understand that relationship. Though something of an idealist, Hourani knew that power and powerlessness could never have an easy relationship. As a young man, he had begun with a strong faith in the 'progressive' role of Britain in the life of the Middle East. He had seen that role as infinitely better than the colonial methods and aims of France. In this he echoed other Arab nationalists, and the British themselves, who believed in the benevolent role of Britain. But he was to be rid of this idealism about the country of his birth within a short time. In one of his memorable essays, 'The Decline of the West in the Middle East', published in 1953, he saw the positions of his country and that of France as identical.

> If we examine the position of England and France in the Arab countries which they controlled or still control, we shall find that it has certain common characteristics. First of all it was imposed by acts of force, and in opposition to such articulate political feeling as existed.
> (Hourani, 1953a: 29)

Imposed by force, this control was always maintained by force, he added. Everything followed from that unequal relation, he believed.

Because of his interest in ideas and the continuity of civilizations, Hourani traced this difficult relationship to the theological tension between Christianity and Islam. The attitude of Christianity toward Islam, he observed, was not the same as that of Islam toward Christianity. Islam, he believed, accepted Christianity as part of its own consciousness. The Prophet

Muhammad had accepted the message of Jesus, while rejecting Jesus's divinity. 'But to the Christian Islam has normally seemed something wholly alien, a distortion of the Christian truth, if not a denial of it, a decline and not a fulfillment' (Hourani, 1953a: 31).

He was to return to this theme repeatedly in his work. In a collection of his essays, published in 1991, the lead essay, 'Islam in European Thought' revisited the issue of Europe's antagonism to Islam. Once again he noted Islam's acceptance of Christianity, and the place of Jesus as 'one of the line of authentic prophets' (Hourani, 1991b: 8). However, Christianity's attitude toward Islam was much more antagonistic:

> For Christians, the matter was more difficult. They knew that Muslims believed in one God, who might be regarded, in his nature and operations, as being the God whom Christians worshipped, but they could not easily accept that Muhammad was an authentic prophet. The event to which Old Testament prophecy had pointed, the coming of Christ, had already taken place; what need was there for further prophets?
>
> (Hourani, 1991b: 8)

Beyond Christianity's antagonism to Islam, Hourani grew convinced that Britain's (and the West's) inability to contribute to the making of a better Middle Eastern political order lay in a problem with the West itself. This is the meaning of the question with which he ended his two-part essay 'The Decline of the West in the Middle East' when he wrote: 'Would there be a "decline of the West in the Middle East" if there were not a "decline of the West"?' (Hourani, 1953a: 183).

Conclusion: The Legacy of an Intellectual Mediator

This question expresses quite well Hourani's disillusionment with the inability of the West to give of itself to other civilizations. This sentiment could be seen in one of his short publications — a pamphlet — entitled *Great Britain and the Arab World*, published in 1946. Here he took Britain to task for the deep distrust its policies had generated in the Arab world. 'Her fundamental defect', he wrote of Britain,

> was that she had nothing to offer the world. Regions within the Empire and States linked to her could expect from her nothing more attractive to the imagination and satisfying to their deeper needs than good order and sanitation. ... Nor did her example any longer bewitch the outer world.
>
> (Hourani, 1946a: 25)

These are harsh words from a scholar who did not write in a particularly harsh way. They reflect the disillusionment with British policy toward Palestine. But that is not all. They also reveal a certain idealistic conception of politics and culture, a belief that power has a responsibility when it deals with powerlessness.

Albert Hourani believed that one civilization could understand the other. He was frustrated with Europe's unwillingness to deal with Islam from a more sympathetic perspective. In a long interview he gave to the Arabic magazine *Al-Majalla* in 1991, he expressed his fear that cultures felt more 'comfortable' with the world when there were enemies to hate, and that Islam was replacing communism as the West's favourite demon.

> I have a feeling now that Islam is the enemy on the

horizon for many in the West, that it is replacing communism as a principal threat. Perhaps this is a subconscious conclusion in the West, but it reflects the view of many. I do not see an end to this antagonism to Islam.

(Nasir, 17–23 April 1991: 60)

It would be erroneous to think that this antagonism was all that Albert Hourani saw in the relationship between Islam and the West. He believed in genuine curiosity, disinterested curiosity about other civilizations. He rejected the idea that Western scholars and students and missionaries went to the Arab world to exercise domination. In tributes to French scholars Louis Massignon and Jacques Berque, and the American historian Marshall Hodgson, he praised the 'Occidental' spirit, its relentless search for knowledge, its genuine curiosity about alien civilizations (see the essays in Hourani, 1991b). What distressed him was the strictly political side of the relationship. And his life and productivity were good examples of what a mind at home in two civilizations could produce.

These are certainly monumental contributions. This does not mean that Hourani's work was flawless and 'complete'. He himself, a modest person, would be the first to acknowledge that there were lacunae in his work, issues that did not concern him or to which he felt unable to make a genuine contribution.

There is, first and foremost, an absence in Hourani's work of that which is 'malignant' and evil in history. Hourani did not appreciate or dwell on what the theologian Reinhold Niebuhr identified as the problem of 'immoral society'. Niebuhr's work suggested that the morality of states is different from that of individuals (Niebuhr, 1932). That important distinction is

Conclusion: The Legacy of an Intellectual Mediator

missing from the analysis in Hourani's work. Hourani did not pursue huge amounts of archival research, and he was not a diplomatic historian. He often took what intellectuals and publicists said at face value. He did not try to 'unmask' men and leaders and policies. Thus his work in its conclusion tended at times to be somewhat bland. He wrote about a violent region, but there was a tranquil tone to his writings. This is why critics such as Daniel Pipes and Martin Kramer, quoted at the beginning of this chapter, could find the ammunition when they wrote about Hourani. Political society, as Niebuhr taught us, could be violent and cruel and immoral and driven by power. This large historical insight is missing from Hourani's work. Perhaps had he done more archival work, he would have had the chance to observe the duplicity of policy. More likely, Hourani knew that policies could be driven by great cruelty, but preferred not to write about it. Either way this omission in his work detracts from the power of what he left us.

A second omission has to do with the sketchy analysis Hourani left us of the decline of the Middle East, relative to the economic and political power of Europe. This theme of decline is quite strong in the writings of Hourani's friend and contemporary, the economic historian Charles Issawi (see Issawi, 1982 and 1983). Issawi delved into the question of decline: the manufacturers who could not compete with European products, the European traders who gained direct access to Middle Eastern cultivators, the insecurity of capital, the Middle Eastern state failing to build infrastructures or to protect markets. These do not figure prominently in Hourani's work. One senses a certain reluctance in him to face the harsh facts of decline. This is a pity because it is only by acknowledging this decline and its realities that it is possible to appreciate the grandeur and success of Islamic civilization when it was at its height. Hourani provided no detailed studies of social and economic decline. The powerlessness against the West to which he returned with great frequency was a product of this decline, yet the decline itself is never directly addressed.

A third problem in Hourani's work has to do with what might be described as the balance between the desert and the Mediterranean in Arab political and social life. He studied the Levant, the coastal cities, but neglected to pay equal attention to the Arabian Peninsula and to the interior and the hinterland. Had he studied the Arabian Peninsula, for example, he would have found a radically different political culture: one less dependent on Europe, more autonomous and organically whole and coherent. Though Hourani studied the 1920s and 1930s, he missed the great political career and drama of 'Abd al-'Aziz Ibn 'Abd al-Rahman al-Sa'ud (Ibn Saud) and the large state in the Peninsula. Deserts shaped a different political culture than the culture of the coastal cities. The Arab world, even that of a country in the Fertile Crescent like Syria, is made of both desert and coastal lands. The balance in Hourani's work is heavily tilted toward the latter.

A fourth problem is also one of relative balance: this one between state and society. Hourani studied Arab society at the expense of studying particular Arab states — their formation, the social and economic bases of their social contract, and their performance. Perhaps this is a by-product of his pan-Arab intellectual orientation. For him the Arab world was one unit, its states too small to stand on their own feet. He preferred to work on a large stage — the Arab world as a whole. Lebanon aside, his work never took up particular Arab countries. The result is that his analysis of the Arab world is at times a bit too abstract and removed from the realities of the states in which Arabs live, and to which they belong.

A fifth omission in his work is the very limited attention he paid after 1973 to the great revolution in Arab life brought about by the new and vast oil wealth. Second only to the coming of Islam into the Arab world, oil wealth changed the foundations of Arab society and its conception of itself. When pressed on this Hourani was given to saying that this was a subject for economic historians like Charles Issawi and Roger Owen (interview with Hourani, Oxford, 14 May 1991). But the 'oil culture' was more than an economic edifice. It also produced a new social and moral and political order. Some Arab societies prospered; others failed. Some social classes did very well while others lost out. The relationship of the state to the society was altered by the oil wealth. So was the relationship of the Arabs to the industrialized world. Of these great changes we get only a very limited appreciation in the work of Albert Hourani. There are only scattered references to the political and psychological drama of oil. We have to turn to other scholars to understand what oil brought to the states of the Arab world. Hourani knew and understood best an older Arab world, the one before the wars of 1967 and 1973, and the mix of great upheaval and great wealth that was brought about by these wars.

None of the above shortcomings can detract from the power and the integrity of Hourani's legacy. He laboured for half a century with great skill: he left what the Arabs would call a *silsila* (a chain of transmission), a school of thought, a method of inquiry to be maintained by his many students and colleagues who were formed by what he wrote and taught. He loved the Arab world and was not apologetic about it. He was a liberal, and never bothered to hide it, or felt that he had to display a tougher side of himself, or to issue harsher judgements of societies and men. He was disillusioned with particular Western policies, but never doubted the great intellectual tradition of the West and its emancipating power.

Albert Hourani died in Oxford, on Sunday, 17 January 1993. His was a rich life, for all his disappointment with what Arab states had done with their independence, and what Britain had done with the power it had in Arab life in the interwar period. The world to which he belonged, and the world that intellectually seized him the most, no longer exists. He was at home in a different political culture, a culture of intellectual elites and great universities, one in which the rulers and the scholars knew and understood one another. He loved the Beirut of the 1950s and 1960s; he would not recognize what it became in the 1980s. He would have been a stranger in the city of radicalism and violence and militiamen. In that older world to which Hourani belonged the Arabs and the West had not yet turned away from one another. What he wrote about George Antonius captures many of the themes in Hourani's own life — its richness, as well as its intellectual tension:

> Anyone who reads *The Arab Awakening* now may end it with a certain feeling of sadness. This is partly a reflection of the anxiety which the author himself felt and expressed. Already by 1938 a shadow of what was to come had fallen across his pages: a new age of mass-politics, when issues would be determined otherwise than by delicate negotiations between men who understood and trusted one another. ... There is another cause of sadness, however. Contemplation of the life of George Antonius will reveal how difficult is the path of the intermediary; he may so easily fall into the chasm he is

Conclusion: The Legacy of an Intellectual Mediator

trying to bridge. His official career showed that he was too large and complex for the kind of intermediate position which was all that was available to an Arab in the mandatory administration; he was squeezed out of the Education Department in a way which reflected little credit on his colleagues. There was, at that time, no other government or institution to which he could give all his talents and devotion. His personal tragedy was that of someone who could not fit easily into any of the moulds available to him at a time when, with the disintegration of ancient societies and systems of government, and the rise of nationalism, men were being forced to define their identities in new and narrower terms. In the last analysis, he belonged to an earlier world: he was a citizen of Alexandria in the last phase of Franco-Ottoman civilisation, the city where all men could be at home, all could be more than one thing, and all matters could be resolved by delicate compromise. He belonged to a world lost and irrecoverable.

'The Arab Awakening Forty Years Later',
in Hourani, 1981: 213–14)

References Cited in the Text

Ajami, Fouad (1978/9) 'The End of Pan-Arabism', *Foreign Affairs*, Winter
— (1981) *The Arab Predicament: Arab Political Thought and Practice Since 1967*, Cambridge/New York: Cambridge University Press
Anglo-American Committee of Inquiry (1946) *Report to the United States Government and His Majesty's Government in the United Kingdom, Lausanne, Switzerland, April 20, 1946*, Washington, DC: United States Government Printer's Office
Antonius, George (1969) *The Arab Awakening: The Story of the Arab National Movement*, New York: G.P. Putnam's Sons (first published 1938)
Arab Office, Washington DC (1946) *The Problem of Palestine*, Washington, DC: Arab Office
Arab Office, London (1947) *The Future of Palestine*, London: Arab Office
Berque, Jacques (1972) *Egypt: Imperialism and Revolution*, London: Faber
Centre for Lebanese Studies (1993) Collection of eulogies on Hourani, 13 March
Crossman, Richard (1947) *Palestine Mission*, London: Hamish Hamilton
Crum, Bartley C. (1947) *Behind the Silken Curtain*, New York: Simon and Schuster Inc.
Dawn, C. Ernest (1973) *From Ottomanism to Arabism*, Urbana, Illinois: University of Illinois Press
Farah, Tawfic (ed.) (1987) *Pan-Arabism and Arab Nationalism: The Continuing Debate*, Boulder, Colorado: Westview Press

Fawaz, Leila (1993) 'In Memoriam: Albert Hourani (1915–1993)', *International Journal of Middle East Studies* 25: 1–12

Gibb, H. A. R. and Harold Bowen (1957) *Islamic Society and the West*, New York/London: Oxford University Press

Haim, Sylvia G. (1962) *Arab Nationalism: An Anthology*, Berkeley: University of California Press

Hourani, Albert (1946a) *Great Britain and the Arab World*, London: J. Murray

— (1946b) *Syria and Lebanon: A Political Essay*, London: Oxford University Press

— (1946c) *Is Zionism the Solution of the Jewish Problem?* Washington, DC: The Arab Office

— (1947) *Minorities in the Arab World* (London/New York: Oxford University Press

— (1949) 'Arab Refugees and the Future of Israel', *Listener*, 7

— (1953a) 'The Decline of the West in the Middle East, Part I', *International Affairs*, January

— (1953b) 'The Decline of the West in the Middle East, Part II', *International Affairs*, April

— (1956) 'Arabic Culture,' in *Perspective of the Arab World*, supplement to *Atlantic Monthly*, October, pp. 5–11

— (1957a) 'Twenty Years of Change', *Middle East Forum*, 32

— (1957b) 'Christians of Lebanon', *Eastern Churches Quarterly*, 12

— (1960) Review of Kamal Salibi, *Maronite History of Medieval Lebanon*, in *Bulletin of the School of Oriental and African Studies*, 23

— (1961) *A Vision of History*, Beirut: Khayats

— (1962a) *Arabic Thought in the Liberal Age, 1789–1939*, Cambridge: Cambridge University Press

— (1962b) 'Musa Alami', *Frontier*, Spring, 319–22

— (1970) 'The Islamic City,' in A. H. Hourani and S. M. Stern (eds) *The Islamic City*, Philadelphia: University of Pennsylvania Press; Oxford: Bruno Cassirer Ltd

— (1980) *Europe and the Middle East*, Berkeley: University of California Press

— (1981) *The Emergence of the Modern Middle East*, Berkeley: University of California Press

— (1986) *Political Society in Lebanon: A Historical Introduction*,

London: Centre for Lebanese Studies
— (ed.) (1988) 'Visions of Lebanon', in Halim Barakat *Toward A Viable Lebanon*, London: Croom Helm
— (1991a) *A History of the Arab Peoples*, Cambridge, Mass.: Harvard University Press
— (1991b) *Islam in European Thought*, Cambridge/New York: Cambridge University Press
— (1991c) 'How Should We Write the History of the Middle East?' *International Journal of Middle East Studies* 23, no. 2 (May)
— (1991d) 'The Achievement of André Raymond', *British Journal of Middle Eastern Studies*, 18 (1) 5–15
— (1991e) Unpublished autobiographical essay, April
Hourani, Albert and J. L. Talmon (1967) *Israel and the Arabs*, London: J. B. Wolters Groningen
Hourani, Cecil (1984) *An Unfinished Odyssey: Lebanon and Beyond*, London: George Weidenfeld and Nicolson
Issawi, Charles (1982) *An Economic History of the Middle East and North Africa*, New York: Columbia University Press
— (1983) 'Why Japan?' in Ibrahim Ibrahim (ed.) *Arab Resources*, London: Croom Helm
Jansen, G. H. (1979) *Militant Islam*, New York: Oxford University Press
Keddie, Nikki R. (1968) *An Islamic Response to Imperialism*, Berkeley: University of California Press
— (1972) *Sayyid Jamal al-Din al-Afghani: A Political Biography*, Berkeley: University of California Press
Kedourie, Elie (1966) *Afghani and Abduh: An Essay on Religious Unbelief and Political Activism in Islam*, New York: Humanities Press
— (1974) *Arabic Political Memoirs and Other Studies*, London: Cass
— (1984) *The Chatham House Version and Other Middle Eastern Studies*, Hanover, NH: published for Brandeis University by the University Press of New England
Khalaf, Samir (1987) *Lebanon's Predicament*, New York: Columbia University Press
Khoury, Philip (1983) *Urban Notables and Arab Nationalism*, Cambridge: Cambridge University Press

Kramer, Martin (1991) 'Giving Order to Despair' (review of *A History of the Arab Peoples*), *Commentary*, 92, September
Lapidus, Ira (1967) *Muslim Cities in the Later Middle Ages* Cambridge, Mass.: Harvard University Press
Lawrence, T. E. (1962) *Seven Pillars of Wisdom*, Middlesex, England: Penguin Books
Lewis, Bernard (1961) *The Emergence of Modern Turkey*, London: Oxford University Press
Louis, Wm. Roger (1984) *The British Empire in the Middle East, 1945–1951*, Oxford: Clarendon Press
Mardin, Serif (1962) *The Genesis of Young Ottoman Thought*, Princeton, NJ: Princeton University Press
Monroe, Elizabeth (1963) *Britain's Moment in the Middle East: 1914–1956*, London: Chatto and Windus
Naff, Thomas (ed.) (1993) in *Paths to the Middle East: Ten Scholars Look Back*, Albany: State University of New York Press
Nasir, Nadim (1991) 'A'lam 'Arab' (Arab luminaries), interview with Albert Hourani, *Al-Majalla*, April
Niebuhr, Reinhold (1932) *Moral Man and Immoral Society: A Study in Ethics and Politics*, New York: Scribner's
Owen, Roger (1993) 'Address Given at the Requiem Mass', St Aloysius Church, Oxford, 25 January
Pipes, Daniel (1991) 'The Arab World from Mohammed Onward' (review of *A History of the Arab Peoples*), *Wall Street Journal*, 5 April
Pitt-Rivers, Julian (ed.) (1963) *Mediterranean Countrymen: Essays in the Social Anthropology of the Mediterranean*, Paris: Mouton
Raymond, André (1985) *The Great Arab Cities in the 16th–18th Centuries*, New York: New York University Press
Reed, Eli and Fouad Ajami (1988) *Beirut: City of Regrets*, New York: W. W. Norton,
Reid, Donald M. (1982) 'Arabic Thought in the Liberal Age Twenty Years After', *International Journal of Middle East Studies*, 14: 541–57
Sadowski, Yahya M. (n.d.) 'The Death of 'Transitional' Syria: Some Remarks Towards the Rebirth of Arab History', unpublished essay
Salibi, Kamal (1965) *The Modern History of Lebanon*, London: Weidenfeld and Nicolson

— (1976) *Crossroads to Civil War: Lebanon, 1958–1976*, Delmar, NY: Caravan Books
— (1981) *A House of Many Mansions: The History of Lebanon Reconsidered*, Berkeley: University of California Press
Tibi, Bassam (1990) *Arab Nationalism: A Critical Inquiry*, New York: St Martin's Press
Toynbee, Arnold (1922) *The Western Question in Greece and Turkey: A Study in the Contact of Civilisations*, London: Constable and Company Limited
— (1987) *A Study of History*, New York/Oxford: Oxford University Press
Wilson, Edmund (1991) *To the Finland Station: A Study in the Writing and Acting of History*, London: Penguin (first published c.1940, London: Secker and Warburg)
Zamir, Meir (1988) *The Formation of Modern Lebanon*, Ithaca, NY: Cornell University Press

Interviews

ISSAWI, Charles. Princeton, New Jersey, 12 June 1991.

FAWAZ, Leila. Cambridge, Massachusetts, 18 June, 1991.

GILSENAN, Michael. Oxford, 17 May 1991.

HOPWOOD, Derek. Oxford, 9 May 1991.

HOURANI, Albert. Washington, DC, 10–11 May 1989; London and Oxford. 6–28 May 1991.

KEDOURIE, Elie. Washington, DC, 17 and 21 February 1992.

KHOURY, Philip. Cambridge, Massachusetts, 19 June 1991.

LEWIS, Bernard. Washington, DC, 3 September 1991.

LOUIS, William Roger. London, 14 May 1991.

MCDOWELL, David. Oxford, 9 May 1991.

OWEN, Roger. Oxford, 16 and 23 May 1991.

PERLMUTTER, Amos. Washington, DC, 5 March 1990.

SADOWSKI, Yahya M. Washington, DC, 12 April 1991.

A Bibliography of Albert Hourani's Published Works[1]
Compiled by Mary C. Wilson

1944
ARTICLE[2]
1. 'Where Shall John Go? V: Syria' in *Horizon*, vol. 9, pp. 424–32.

1945
PAMPHLET
1. *The Arabs and Western Civilization*. Khartoum, Sudan Cultural Centre, 13 pp.

1946
BOOK
1. *Syria and Lebanon*. London, Oxford University Press, 402 pp.

---

1. Mary C. Wilson acknowledges her gratitude to the *International Journal of Middle East Studies* and to the Cambridge University Press for permission to reprint this revised version of the bibliography that appeared in volume 16 (1984) of the journal.
2. Subsequent editions of published worksk are included only when significant changes have been made in content or format.

PAMPHLETS

2. *Is Zionism the Solution of the Jewish Problem?* London, Arab Office, 8 pp.
3. *Great Britain and the Arab World.* London, John Murray, 46 pp.
4. *The Problem of Palestine.* Washington, DC, The Arab Office

ARTICLES

5. 'Al-'Arab wa'l-Madaniyya al-Gharbiyya' in *Al-Abhath* (Beirut), vol. 6, pp. 3–18. [Translation of *The Arabs and Western Civilization*, see 1945, entry 1]
6. 'New Trends in Arab Politics' in *The Times* (London), 12 August.
7. 'Discussion: A. Koestler's *Thieves in the Night*' in *Tribune*, 6 December, pp. 20–I.
7. 'Revival of the Arab Mind' in *Asia and the Americas*, March, pp. 122–5.

1947

BOOK

1. *Minorities in the Arab World.* London, Oxford University Press, 140 pp.
2. *The Failure of Palestine.* Geneva, Impimerie Centrale (substantially written by A. Hourani.)

ARTICLES

3. 'The Arab World and Russia' in *New Statesman*, 28 January, pp. 468–9.
4. 'Den arabiska enhetsrörelson' [The Movement for Arab Unity] in *Utrikes Politik* (Stockholm), vol. 2, pp. 92–101.

REVIEWS

5. J. Lavrin, *Pushkin and Russian Literature*, and N. Gogol, *The Government Inspector* in *Tribune*, 13 June, pp. 15–16.
6. H. Fyfe, *The Illusion of National Character* in *Tribune*, 13 June, p. 16.

7. R. Fedden, *Syria* in *Horizon*, vol. 15, pp. 374–7.
8. N. Barbour, *Nisi Dominus* in *International Affairs*, vol. 27, pp. 132–3.

1949

ARTICLE

1. 'Arab Refugees and the Future of Israel' in *Listener*, 28 July, pp. 134 ff.

1950

ARTICLES

1. 'Syria and Lebanon' in Royal Institute of International Affairs, *The Middle East: A Political and Economic Survey*. London, Oxford University Press, pp. 383–417.
2. 'British Policy in the Fertile Crescent' in *United Empire*, vol. 41, 211–16.
3. 'Al-'Alam al-'Arabi wa'l-Mustaqbal' [The Arab World and the Future] in *Al-Mustami 'al-'Arabi* (London), vol. 11, no. 3, pp. 3 and 26, and no. 4, pp. 4–5.

REVIEW

4. H. A. R. Gibb and H. Bowen, *Islamic Society and the West* (vol. 1, part 1) in *International Affairs*, vol. 26, pp. 533–4.

1951

ARTICLES

1. Un quartier copte du Vieux-Caire' in *La Femme Nouvelle* (Cairo), Summer, pp. 72–80.
2. 'The Levant' in *Aramco World*, vol. 2, pp. 2–4.

REVIEWS

3. M. Gaudefroy-Demombynes, *Muslim Institutions in International Affairs*, vol. 27, pp. 56–7.

4. A. Pallis, *In the Days of the Janissaries* in *Egyptian Gazette* (Cairo), 2 July.

1952

ARTICLES

1. 'Islam and the West' in *Listener*, vol. 25, pp. 501–2.
2. [Anon.] 'Faris Nimr Pasha' in *Journal of the Royal Central Asian Society*, vol. 39, pp. 167–9.

1953

ARTICLES

1. 'The Decline of the West in the Middle East' in *International Affairs* vol. 29, pp. 22 ff.
2. 'Muslims and Christians' in *Christian Newsletter*, vol. 1, pp. 179–86.

REVIEWS

3. G. Kirk, *The Middle East in the War* in *International Affairs*, vol. 29, pp. 204–5.
4. E. Jackh, *Background of the Middle East* in *International Affairs*, vol. 29, p. 517.
5. W. J. Fischel, *Ibn Khaldun and Tamerlane* in *English Historical Review*, vol. 68, pp. 134–5.
6. M. Shibeika, *British Policy in the Sudan* in *African Affairs*, vol. 52, pp. 166–7.

1954

ARTICLE

1. 'Tadahwur al-Gharb fi'l-Sharq al-Awsat' in *Al-Abhath* (Beirut), vol. 8, pp. 361–437. [Translation of 'The Decline of the West in the Middle East', see 1953, entry 1]

REVIEWS

2. F. Sayegh, *Understanding the Arab Mind* in *International Affairs*, vol. 30, p. 114.
3. S. H. Longrigg, *Iraq 1900–1950* in *Middle East Journal*, vol.8, pp. 341–2.
4. A. K. S. Lambton, *Landlord and Peasant in Persia* in *Islamic Quarterly*, vol. 1, pp. 65–6.
5. United Nations, *Review of Economic Conditions in the Middle East* in *Islamic Quarterly*, vol. 1, pp. 67–8.

1955

ARTICLES

1. 'Race and Related Ideas in the Near East' in A. W. Lind, ed., *Race Relations in World Perspective*. Honolulu, University of Hawaii Press, pp. 116–44. [Reprinted with revisions in 1961, entry 1]
2. 'The Concept of Race Relations: Thoughts after a Conference' in *International Social Science Bulletin*, vol. 7, pp. 335–340. [Reprinted with revisions in 1961, entry 1]
3. 'Toynbee's Vision of History' in *Dublin Review*, vol. 119, pp. 375–401. [Reprinted with revisions in 1961, entry 1; and 1879, entry 1]
4. 'The Anglo-Egyptian Agreement: Some Causes and Implications' in *Middle East Journal*, vol. 9, pp. 239–55.
5. 'The Vanishing Veil' in *UNESCO Courier*, vol. 8, pp. 35–7.

REVIEWS

6. G. Kirk, *The Middle East 1945–1950* in *International Affairs*, vol. 31, pp. 71–5.
7. P. Mason, *An Essay on Racial Tension* in *International Affairs*, vol. 31, pp. 81–3.
8. I. S. O. Playfair et al., *The Mediterranean and the Middle East* (vol. 1) in *International Affairs*, vol. 31, pp. 96–7.

1956

ARTICLES

1. 'Arabic Culture' in *Perspective of the Arab World*, supplement to *Atlantic Monthly*, October, pp. 5–11.
2. Introduction to M. S. Agwani, *The United States and the Arab World*. Aligarh, Institute of Islamic Studies.

REVIEWS

3. H. P. Hall and A. W. Noyes, eds., *Current Research on the Middle East, 1955* in *International Affairs*, vol. 32, pp. 382–3.
4. L. Massignon, ed., *Annuaire du Monde Musulman* in *International Affairs*, vol. 32, p. 383.
5. N. Faris and M. T. Husayn, *The Crescent in Crisis* in *International Affairs*, vol. 32, pp. 384–5.
6. E. Kedourie, *England and the Middle East* in *International Affairs*, vol. 32, pp. 511–12.
7. I. S. O. Playfair et al., *The Mediterranean and the Middle East* (vol. 2) in *International Affairs*, vol. 32, p. 484.

1957

ARTICLES

1. 'The Changing Face of the Fertile Crescent in the Eighteenth Century' in *Studia Islamica*, vol. 8, pp. 89–122. [Reprinted with revisions in 1961, entry 1]
2. 'Twenty Years of Change' in *Middle East Forum*, vol. 32, pp. 7ff.
3. Christians of Lebanon' in *Eastern Churches Quarterly*, vol. 12, pp. 135–44.
4. 'Al-Sharq al-Adna-'Ahsrun 'Aman min al-Tatawwur' in *Al-Abhath* (Beirut), vol. 10, pp. 307–28. [Translation of 'Twenty Years of Change,' see 1957, entry 2]

REVIEWS

5. J. Morris, *The Market of Seleukia* in *Observer*, 10 November.

1958

ARTICLES

1. 'The Pull of Arab Unity' in *The Times* (London), 21 and 22 May.
2. 'The Middle East and the Crisis of 1956' in *St. Antony's Papers 4: Middle Eastern Affairs 1*, pp. 9–42. London, Chatto and Windus. [Reprinted with revisions in 1961, entry 1)
3. 'Christians in the Arab World' in *Frontier*, vol. 1, pp. 265–70.
4. 'Syria' in R. Bullard, ed., *The Middle East: A Political and Economic Survey*. London, Oxford University Press, pp. 450–87.

REVIEWS

5. H. A. R. Gibb and H. Bowen, *Islamic Society and the West* (vol. 1, part 2), in *International Affairs*, vol. 34, pp. 201–2.
6. W. Cantwell Smith, *Islam in Modern History* in *Bulletin of the School of Oriental and African Studies*, vol. 21, pp. 633–5.
7. T. Little, *Egypt*, and J. and S. Lacouture, *Egypt in Transition* in *Observer*, 23 November.

1959

ARTICLES

1. 'The Regulative Principle' in *Democracy in the New States*. New Delhi, Congress for Cultural Freedom, pp. 147–164. [Reprinted with revisions in 1961, entry 1]
2. 'Aspectos del mundo islamico' in *Cuadernos* [Paris], supplement to no. 34. [Translation of 'The Regulative Principle,' see 1959, entry 1]
3. 'La loi islamique et les problèmes de l'état moderne' in *Preuves* [Paris], vol. 97, pp. 36–41. [Translation of 'The Regulative Principle', see 1959, entry 1]
4. 'The Future of Foreign Universities in the Middle East' in *Science and Freedom*, vol. 13, pp. 23–9.
5. 'Mustaqbal al-Jami'at al-Ajnabiyya fi'1-Sharq al-Aivsat' in *Al-Fikr* [Tunis], vol. 5. [Translation of 'The Future of Foreign Universities in the Middle East,' see 1959, entry 4]

REVIEW

6. D. Landes, *Bankers and Pashas* in *English Historical Review*, vol. 74, pp.745–6.

1960

ARTICLES

1. Preface to J. M. Ahmad, *The Intellectual Origins of Egyptian Nationalism*. London, Oxford University Press, pp. vii–xi.
2. 'Revolutionary Nationalism' in K. A. Jelenski, ed., *History and Hope*. London, Routledge and Kegan Paul, pp. 101–7.
3. 'Le nationalisme revolutionnaire' in *Preuves*, vol. 116, pp. 59–62. [Translation of 'Revolutionary Nationalism,' see 1960, entry 2]
4. 'El nacionalismo revolucionario' in *Cuardernos*, supplement to no.45, pp. 17–19. [Translation of 'Revolutionary Nationalism,' see 1960, entry 2]
5. 'Christians and Muslims' in *Frontier*, vol. 3, pp. 127–132. [Reprinted with revisions in 1980, entry 1]

REVIEWS

6. K. Salibi, *Maronite Historians of Medjaeval Lebanon* in *Bulletin of the School of Oriental and African Studies*, vol. 23, pp. 395–6.
7. R. Landau, *Islam and the Arabs* in *Muslim World*, vol. 50, pp. 55–6.
8. R. Hill, *Egypt in the Sudan* in *English Historical Review*, vol.75, p. 541.
9. S. N. Fisher, *The Middle East* in *English Historical Review*, vol. 75, pp. 713–14.
10. Z. N. Zeine, *The Struggle for Arab Independence* in *Middle East Forum*, vol. 36, p. 41.

1961

BOOKS

1. *A Vision of History*. Beirut, Khayats, 160 pp. [Includes with revisions; 1955, entries 1, 2, and 3; 1957, entry 1; 1958, entry 2; and 1959, entry 1]

2. [Ed.] *St Antony's Papers 11: Middle Eastern Affairs* 2. London, Chatto and Windus, 167 pp.

REVIEWS

3. Sir R. Bullard, *The Camels Must Go* in *Telegraph*, 7 May.
4. F. Stark, *Dust in the Lion's Paw* in *Telegraph*, 8 October.

1962

BOOK

1. *Arabic Thought in the Liberal Age, 1798–1939.* London, Oxford University Press, 403 pp.

ARTICLES

2. [Anon.] 'Musa Alami' in *Frontier*, vol. 5, pp. 319–22.
3. 'Historians of Lebanon' in B. Lewis and P. M. Holt, eds, *Albert Hourani's Published Works Historians of the Middle East*. London, Oxford University Press, pp. 226–45. [Reprinted with revisions in 1981, entry 1]
4. 'General Themes: Introductory Remarks' in 1962, entry 3, pp. 451–6.
5. 'Taha Husayn: Tafkiruhu al-Ijtima'i' in *Himar* [Beirut], vol. 1, pp. 61–70. [Translation of chapter 12 of 1961, entry 1]
6. 'The Life and Ideas of Wilfred Scawen Blunt' in *Middle East Forum*, vol. 38, pp. 21–7. [Reprinted with revisions in 1980, entry 1]
7. 'Professor Louis Massignon' in *The Times* (London), 21 November.
8. 'Djam'iyya' in *Encyclopaedia of Islam*, 2nd ed., vol. 2, pp. 428–9.

REVIEW

9. P. M. Holt, *A Modern History of the Sudan* in *Bulletin of the School of Oriental and African Studies*, vol. 25, pp. 359–60.

1963

BOOK

1. [Ed.] *St Antony's Papers 16: Middle Eastern Affairs 3*. London, Chatto and Windus, 184 pp.

ARTICLES

2. 'Near Eastern Nationalism Yesterday and Today' in *Foreign Affairs*, vol. 42, pp. 123–6. [Reprinted with revisions in 1981, entry 1]
3. 'The Decline of the West in the Middle East' in R. N. Nolte, ed., *The Modern Middle East*. New York, Atherton Press, pp. 30–56. [Reprint of part 1 of 1953, entry 1]
4. 'Hashim al-Atasi' in *Encyclopaedia Britannica*, vol. 2, p. 663.

REVIEW

5. E. Wakin, *A Lonely Minority* in *Middle East Journal*, vol. 17, pp. 323–5.

1964

ARTICLES

1. [Anon.] 'Mr Edward Atiyah' in *The Times* (London), 26 October. Reproduced in *Bulletin of the Republic of Iraq*, vol. 5, pp. 2–3.

REVIEWS

2. B. Lewis, *The Middle East and the West* in *Telegraph*, 17 May.
3. G. Baer, *Population and Society in the Arab East* in *Oxford Magazine*, 21 May.
4. H. Ingrams, *The Yemen*, and A. Hottinger, *The Arabs* in *New Statesman*, 5 June.

1965

BOOK

1. [Ed.] *St Antony's Papers 19: Middle Eastern Affairs 4*. London, Oxford University Press, 165 pp.

REVIEWS

2. E. Stillman and W. Pfaff, *The Politics of Hysteria* in *Observer*, 7 February.
3. J. Sauvaget, *Introduction to the History of the Muslim East* in *Middle East Forum*, vol. 41, pp. 92–3.

1966

ARTICLES

1. 'Syria and Lebanon: Arab Nationalism' in I. Wallerstein, ed., *Social Change: the Colonial Situation*. New York, John Wiley and Sons, pp.551–8. [Reprinted from 1946; entry 1]
2. 'Lebanon from feudalism to modern state' in *Middle Eastern Studies*, vol. 2, pp. 256–63. [Reprinted with revisions in 1981, entry 1]
3. 'Lebanon: The Development of a Political Society' in L. Binder, ed. *Politics in Lebanon*. New York, John Wiley and Sons, pp. 13–29. [Reprinted with revisions in 1981, entry 1]
4. 'Independence and the Imperial Legacy' in *Middle East Forum*, vol. 47, pp. 5–27.
5. 'Damascus: History, Islamic and Modern' in *Encyclopaedia Britannica*, vol. 7, pp. 23–4.
6. 'Shukri al-Kuwatli' in *Encyclopaedia Britannica*, vol. 13, p. 521.
7. 'Lebanon: History' in *Encyclopaedia Britannica*, vol. 13, pp. 875–6.

REVIEWS

8. U. Gehrke and G. Kuhn, *Die Grenzen des Irak* in *English Historical Review*, vol. 81, p. 445.
9. J. H. Proctor, ed., *Islam and International Relations* in *Middle East Journal*, vol. 20, pp. 114–116.
10. D. Holden, *Farewell to Arabia* in *Sunday Times* (London), 10 July.
11. K. S. al-Husry, *Three Reformers: A Study in Modern Arab Political Thought* in *Middle East Forum*, vol. 47, pp. 109–10.

1967

BOOKS

1. *Arabic Thought in the Liberal Age.* London, Oxford University Press. [Reprint of 1962, entry 1 with new preface]
2. *Israel and the Arab.* London: J. B. Wolter Groningen (with J. L. Talmon).

ARTICLES

3. 'Islam and the Philosphers of History' in *Middle Eastern Studies,* vol. 3, pp. 206–68. [Reprinted with revisions in 1980, entry 1]
4. 'Palestine and Israel' in *Observer*, 3 September.
5. 'Palestine and Israel' in *Middle East Forum,* vol. 43, pp. 21–7. [Reprint of 1967, entry 3 with some changes]
6. Arabic translation of parts of 'Palestine and Israel' in *Ruz al-Yusuf* [Cairo], 18 September, pp. 16–17. [See 1967, entry 3]

1968

BOOK

1. *Syria and Lebanon.* Beirut, Librairie du Liban. [Reprint of 1946, entry 1]

ARTICLES

2. 'Ottoman Reform and the Politics of Notables' in W. R. Polk and R. L. Chambers, eds., *Beginnings of Modernization in the Middle East: the Nineteenth Century.* Chicago, University of Chicago Press, pp. 41–68. [Reprinted with revisions in 1981, entry 1]
3. 'Palestine and Israel' in M. Khadduri, ed., *The Arab-Israeli Impasse.* Washington, R. B. Luce, pp. 157–65. [Reprint of 1967, entry 3]

REVIEWS

4. E. I. J. Rosenthal, *Islam in the Modern National State* in *Middle Eastern Studies,* vol. 4, pp. 108–11.
5. [Anon.] B. Lewis, *The Assassins* in *Economist,* 6 January.

6. [Anon.] S. D. Goitein, *A Mediterranean Society* in *Economist*, 10 August.
7. P. M. Holt, *Egypt and the Fertile Crescent, 1516–1922* in *English Historical Review*, vol. 83, pp. 393–4.
8. A. L. Tibawi, *American Interests in Syria 1800–1901* in *English Historical Review*, vol. 83, pp. 626–7.
9. N. Daniel, *Islam, Europe and Empire* in *Middle Eastern Studies*, vol. 4, pp. 325–6.
10. A. S. Atiyya, *A History of Eastern Christianity* in *New Blackfriars*, vol. 49, pp. 660–1.
11. J. J. Waardenburg, *Les universités dans le monde arabe actuel* in *British Journal of Educational Studies*, vol. 16, pp. 332–3.

1969

ARTICLES

1. 'Comment' in *The Gulf: Implications of British Withdrawal*. Washington, Centre for Strategic and International Studies, Georgetown University, pp. 15–17.
2. 'The Development of Middle Eastern Studies at Oxford 1962–1968'. *Oriental, Slavonic, East European and African Studies*, supplement 10 to *Oxford University Gazette*, vol. 99, pp. 6–14.
3. 'Palestine and Israel' in W. Z. Laqueur, ed., *Arab-Israel Reader*. London, Weidenfeld and Nicolson, pp. 273–80. [Reprint of 1967, entry 3]

REVIEWS

4. J. Nevakivi, *Britain, France and the Middle East, 1914–1920* in *Spectator*, 14 March.
5. G. Furlonge, *Palestine is My Country: The Story of Musa Alami* in *Frontier*, vol. 2, pp. 238–9.
6. [Anon.] P. Knightley and C. Simpson, *The Secret Lives of Lamrence of Arabia* in *Economist*, 4 October.
7. P. M. Holt, ed., *Political and Social Change in Modern Egypt* in *English Historical Review*, vol. 48, pp. 865–6.

8. J. B. Kelly, *Britain and the Persian Gulf* in *Historical Journal*, vol. 12, pp. 334–5.

1970

BOOKS

1. [Ed. with S. M. Stern] *The Islamic City*. Oxford, Bruno Cassirer, and Philadelphia, University of Pennsylvania Press, 222 pp.
2. *Arabic Thought in the Liberal Age*. London, Oxford University Press. [Paperback edition of 1967, entry 1]

PAMPHLET

3. *The Ottoman Background of the Modern Middle East* [Third Carreras Arab Lecture of the University of Essex]. London, Longman, 20 pp. and Arabic translation, 26 pp. [Reprinted with revisions in 1981, entry 1]

ARTICLES

4. 'The Islamic city in the light of recent research' in 1970, entry 1, pp. 9–24. [Reprinted with revisions in 1981, entry 1]
5. 'Fees for overseas students' in *Oxford University Gazette*, supplement 2, 22 June, pp. 1293–5.
6. 'Funeral Oration' in *Samuel Miklos Stern*, pp. 3–6. Oxford, All Souls College, privately printed.

REVIEWS

7. N. Keddie, *An Islamic Response to Imperialism* in *International Journal of Middle East Studies*, vol. 1, pp. 90–1.
8. O. Chadwick, *The Victorian Church*, and E. Isichei, *Victorian Quakers* in *Spectator*, 30 May.
9. J. A. Field, *America and the Mediterranean World 1776–1882* in *English Historical Review*, vol. 85, pp. 861–2.

1971

REVIEWS

1. [Anon.] Al-Jabarti, *Merveilles biographiques et historiques* in *Times Literary Supplement*, 19 February.
2. M. A. Cook, ed., *Studies in the Economic History of the Middle East* in *Economic History Review*, vol. 29, pp. 510–11.

1972

BOOK

1. [Ed. with S. M. Stern and V. Brown] *Islamic Philosphy and the Classical Tradition*. Oxford, Bruno Cassirer, 549 pp.

ARTICLES

2. 'Shaikh Khalid and the Naqshbandi Order' in 1972, entry pp. 83–103. [Reprinted with revisions in 1981, entry 1]
3. 'Revolution in the Arab Middle East' in P. J. Vatikiotis, ed., *Revolution in the Middle East*. London, George Allen and Unwin, pp. 65–72. [Reprinted with revisions in 1981, entry 1]
4. 'Foreword' to J. Berque, *Egypt, Imperialism and Revolution*. London, Faber and Faber, pp. 5–7.
5. Preface to A. Schölch, *Agypten den Agyptern!* Zurich, Atlantis Verlag, pp. 9–13.

REVIEWS

6. R. M. Haddad, *Syrian Christians in Muslim Society* in *Journal of Theological Studies*, vol. 29, p. 267.
7. P. M. Holt, B. Lewis and A. K. S. Lambton, eds., *The Cambridge History of the Middle East* in *English Historical Review,*, vol. 87, pp.348–57.

1973

ARTICLE

1. 'The Syrians in Egypt in the eighteenth and nineteenth centuries'

in *Colloque international sur l'histoire du Caire.* Cairo, Ministry of Culture, pp. 221–33. [Reprinted with revisions in 1981, entry 1]

REVIEWS

2. H. Lewis, *Islam in History* in *Journal of Jewish Studies,* vol. 24, pp. 196–7.
3. N. Keddie, *Sayyid Jamal al-Din 'al-Afghani'* in *International Journal of Middle East Studies,* vol. 5, pp. 492–5.
4. M. Rodinson, *Marxisme et monde musulman* in *Journal of Semitic Studies,* vol. 28, pp. 318–19.

1974

PAMPHLET

1. *Western Attitudes towards Islam* [Tenth Montefiore Memorial Lecture] University of Southampton, 22 pp. [Reprinted with revisions in 1980, entry 1]

ARTICLES

2. 'Sir Hamilton Gibb' in *Proceedings of the British Academy.* London, Published for the British Academy by the Oxford University Press, vol. 58, pp. 493–521. [Reprinted with revisions in 1980, entry 1]
3. 'The Ottoman background of the modern Middle East' in K. H. Karpat, ed., *The Ottoman Empire and its Place in World History.* Leiden, E. J. Brill, pp.61–78. [[Reprint of 1970, entry 3 with changes, reprinted with revisions in 1981, entry 1]
4. 'Presidential Address' in *Bulletin of the British Society for Middle Eastern Studies,* vol. 1, pp. 47–50.

1975

ARTICLE

1. 'Presidential Address' in *Bulletin of the British Society for Middle Eastern Studies,* vol. 2, pp. 65–9.

1976

ARTICLES

1. 'The Common Language of Islam' in *Observer*, 16 May.
2. 'Ideologies of the Mountain and the City' in R. Owen, ed., *Essays on the Crisis in Lebanon*. London, Ithaca Press, pp. 33–41. [Reprinted with revisions in 1981, entry 1]
3. 'Reflections on the Present State of Islamic Historiography' in J. Berque and D. Chevallier, eds., *Les Arabes par leurs archives (XVIe–XXe siècles)*. Paris, Edition du CNRS, pp. 19–27. [Reprinted with revisions in 1980, entry 1]
4. 'History' in L. Binder, ed., *The Study of the Middle East*. New York, John Wiley and Sons, pp. 97–135.
5. 'Foreword' to P. J. Sluglett, *Britain in Iraq, 1919–1932*. London, Ithaca Press.
6. 'Lebanon, Syria, Jordan and Iraq' in A. L. Udovitch, ed., *The Middle East: Oil, Conflict and Hope*. Lexington, MA., D. C. Heath, pp.269–290.
7. 'Nash'at al-Qawmiyya al-'Arabiyya' [The Origins of Arab Nationalism] in I. Ibrahim, ed., *Dirasat fi'l Iqtisad zea'l-Siyasa zva'l-Qanun*. Abu Dhabi, Ministry of Foreign Affairs, pp. 113–28.

REVIEWS

8. G. Scholem, *Sabbatai Sevi, the Mystical Messiah, 1626–1676* in *Journal of Jewish Studies*, vol. 27, pp. 96–102.
9. J. Schacht with C. E. Bosworth, *The Legacy of Islam* in *Journal of Semitic Studies*, vol. 21, pp. 217–21.

1977

ARTICLES

1. 'Aspects of Islamic Culture: Introduction' in T. Naff and R. Owen, eds., *Studies in Eighteenth Century Islamic History*. Carbondale, Illinois, Southern Illinois University Press, pp. 253–76.
2. 'Rashid Rida and the Sufi Orders: a Footnote to Laoust' in *Bulletin d'Etudes Orientales*, vol. 29, pp. 231–41. [Reprinted with revisions in 1981; entry 1.]

3. 'Foreword' to J. P. Spagnolo, *France and Ottoman Lebanon, 1861–1914*. London, Ithaca Press.

REVIEW

4. D. Stewart, T. E. Lawrence in *Observer*, 24 July.

1978

ARTICLES

1. 'Moh'ammed 'Abduh' in C. A. Julien, ed., *Les Africains*, vol. 10. Paris, Editions J. A., pp. 37–71.
2. 'Foreword' to S. Bakhash, *Iran: Monarchy, Bureaucracy and Reform under the Qajars,1858–1896*. London, Ithaca Press.

REVIEWS

3. M. Hodgson, *The Venture of Islam* in *Journal of Near Eastern Studies*, vol. 37, pp. 53–62.
4. B. Lewis, *Islam from the Prophet Muhammad to the Capture of Constantinople* in *English Historical Review*, vol. 93, p. 425.

1979

ARTICLES

1. 'What is an "Islamic Nation"?' in *Newsday*, 21 February.
2. 'Syria and Lebanon' in D. Grimwood-Jones, ed., *The Middle East and Islam*. Zug, Switzerland, Inter-Documentation Company, pp. 325–32.
3. 'Foreword' to M. Deeb, *Party Politics in Egypt: the Wafd and its Rivals, 1919–1939*. London, Ithaca Press.

REVIEWS

4. E. Said, *Orientalism* in *New York Review of Books*, 8 March.
5. K. L. Brown, *People of Salé* in *Journal of Semitic Studies*, vol. 24, pp.153–4.

1980

BOOK

1. *Europe and the Middle East.* London, Macmillan Press, and Berkeley, University of California Press, 226 pp. [Includes, with revisions: 1955, entry 3; 1960, entry 5; 1962, entry 6; 1967, entry 2; 1974, entries 1 and 2; 1976, entry 3]

ARTICLES

2. 'Foreword' to R. I. Khalidi, *British Policy towards Syria and Palestine, 1906–1914.* London, Ithaca Press.
3. 'Islamic History, Middle Eastern History, Modern History' in M. H. Kerr, ed., *Islamic Studies: a Tradition and its Problems.* Malibu, Calif., Undena Publications, pp. 5–26.
4. 'Volney and the Ruin of Empires' in 1980, entry 1, pp. 81–6.

REVIEW

5. M. A. Boisard, *L'Humanisme de l'Islam* in *Maghreb Review,* vol. 5, pp. 37–8.

1981

BOOK

1. *The Emergence of the Modern Middle East.* London, Macmillan Press, and Berkeley, University of California Press, 243 pp. [Includes with revisions, 1962, entry 3; 1963, entry 2; 1966, entries 2 and 3; 1968, entry 2; 1970, entries 3 and 4; 1972, entries 2 and 3; 1973, entry 1; 1976, entry 2; 1977, entry 2]

ARTICLES

2. 'Foreword' to A. Scholch, *Egypt for the Egyptians!* London, Ithaca Press.
3. 'Al-Hilal al-Khasib fi'l-Qarn al- Thamin 'Ashar' in *Al-Waqi'* (Beirut), vol. 1, no. 1, pp. 45–76. [Translation of 'The Changing Face of the Fertile Crescent in the Eighteenth Century,' see 1957, entry 1]

4. 'The Arab Awakening, Forty Years Later' in 1981, entry 1, pp. 193–215.

REVIEWS

5. M. Larès, *T. E. Lawrence, la France et les Français* in *Times Literary Supplement*, 29 May.
6. R. Peters, *Islam and Colonialism* in *Maghreb Review*, vol. 6, p. 40.
7. M. Ayoub, ed., *The Middle East in World Affairs* in *Maghreb Review*, vol. 6, p. 43.

1982

ARTICLES

1. 'In Search of a New Andalusia: Jacques Berque and the Arabs' in C. Hourani, ed., *The Arab Cultural Scene*, supplement to *Literary Review*, pp. 7–11.
2. 'Conclusions' in Groupe de Recherches et d'Etudes sur le Proche Orient, *L'Egypte au XIXe siècle*. Paris, Editions du CNRS, pp. 329–34.
3. 'Foreword' to M. A. Tarbush, *The Role of the Military in Politics: a Case Study of Iraq to 1941*. London, Kegan Paul International.
4. [Anon.] 'Dr Hamid Enayat' in *The Times* (London), 3 August.
5. 'Qira'a fi'l-istishraq' in *Al-Turath al-'Arabi* (Damascus), vol.2, pp. 164–71. [Translation of 1979, entry 4]
6. 'Al-Islah al-'Uthmani wa'l-Mashriq al-'Arabi' in *Al-Waqi'* (Beirut), vol. 1, no. 4, pp. 59–92. [Translation of 'Ottoman Reform and the Politics of Nationalism', see 1968, entry 2]

REVIEWS

7. C. M. Andrew and A. S. Kanya-Forstner, *France Overseas* in *Times Literary Supplement*, 22 January.
8. J. Ninet, *Lettres d'Egypte 1870–1882* in *Welt des Islams*, vol. 20, pp. 229–30.
9. C. V. Findley, *Bureaucratic Reform in the Ottoman Empire: the Sublime Porte 1789–1922* in *Journal of Modern History*, vol. 54, pp. 194–7.

1983

BOOK

1. *Arabic Thought in the Liberal Age.* Cambridge, Cambridge University Press, 406 pp. [Paperback edition with new preface and supplementary bibliography to 1962, entry 1]

ARTICLES

2. 'T. E. Lawrence and Louis Massignon' in *Times Literary Supplement*, 8 July, pp. 733–4.
3. 'Conclusion' to J. Piscatori, ed., *Islam in the Political Process.* Cambridge, Cambridge University Press, pp. 226–34.
4. 'Conclusion' to A. Dawisha, ed., *Islam in Foreign Policy.* Cambridge, Cambridge University Press, pp. 178–81.
5. [Anon.] 'Richard P. Mitchell' in *The Times* (London), 20 September.
6. 'Al-Istishraq–Mustashriqun: Hamilton Gibb: Injazat Mustashriq' in *Al-Fihr al-'Arabi* (Beirut), vol. 13, pp. 373–98. [Translation of 'Sir Hamilton Gibb', see 1974, entry 2]

1984

ARTICLES

1. 'Middle Eastern Studies Today' in *Bulletin of the British Society for Middle Eastern Studies*, vol. 11, pp. 111–20.
2. 'Asad Rustum's *Corpus of Arabic Document*' in *Asad Rustum, al-Insan ma al-Mu'arrikh* Beirut, Al-Maktaba al-Bulusiyya, pp. 42–8, followed by an Arabic translation on pp. 51–6.

REVIEWS

3. Charles A. Frazee, *Catholics and Sultans: The Church and the Ottoman Empire 1453–1923* in *The Tablet* (London), 16 June, pp. 292–3.
4. Jacques Berque, *Arab Rebirth* in *Middle East International*, 20 April, p. 18.

5. Marc Ferro, *The Use and Abuse of History* in *The Tablet*, 16 June, pp. 580–1.
6. Gordon Brook-Shepherd, *Victims at Sarajevo* in *The Tablet*, 18 August, p. 796.

1985

ARTICLE

1. 'Foreword' to L. Schatowski-Schilcher, *Families in* Weisbaden/Stuttgart, Franz Steiner Verlag, pp. vii–viii.

REVIEW

2. B. Lewis, *The Jews of Islam* and J. Peters, *From Time Immemorial* in *Observer*, 3 March, p. 27.

1986

BOOK

1. *Arabic Thought in the Liberal Age 1798–1939*. [Reprint of 1983, entry 1]

PAMPHLETS

2. *Elizabeth Monroe, CMG, wife of Humphrey Neame, FRCS*. Address at the Service of Thanksgiving at West Hendred Church, 7 pp.
3. *Political Society in Lebanon: A Historical Introduction* (Inaugural lecture of the Emile Bustani Middle East Seminar). Cambridge, Center for International Studies, Massachusetts Institute of Technology and Oxford, Centre for Lebanese Studies, 16 pp.

ARTICLES

4. 'From Jabal Amil to Persia' in *Bulletin of the School of Oriental and African Studies*, vol. 45, pp. 133–40.
5. 'Foreword' to P. Seale, *The Struggle for Syria: a study of post-war Arab politics*. London, I.B.Tauris.
6. 'Gibb, Sir H. A. R.' in *Dictionary of National Biography*. Oxford, Oxford University Press, pp. 336–7.

7. 'Al-mutjama' al-siyasi fi Lubnan' in *Al-Safir* (Beirut), 21 and 28 October. [Arabic translation of entry 3 above]
8. 'Hijret 'ulama-i Shi'a az Jabal 'Amil bi Iran' in *Kayhan Farhangi*, November, pp. 13–16. [Persian translation of 1986, entry 4]

REVIEWS

9. E. Toledano, *The Ottoman Slave Trade and its Suppression* in *English Historical Review*, vol. 101, pp. 281–3.
10. Y. Porath, *In Search of Arab Unity* in *Times Literary Supplement*, 21 November, pp. 1297–8.

1987

ARTICLES

1. 'Foreword' to Philip S. Khoury, *Syria and the French Mandate*. Princeton, Princeton University Press and London, I.B.Tauris, pp. xi–xii.
2. 'T. E. Lawrence and Louis Massignon' in Daniel Massignon, ed. *Presence de Louis Massignon*. Paris, Maisonneuve et Larose, pp. 167–76. [Reprint of 1983, entry 2]
3. 'Jamal al-Din al-Afghani' in M. Eliade, ed., *Encyclopedia of Religion*. New York, Macmillan, vol. 1, pp. 59–60.
4. 'Rashid Rida', in *Encyclopedia of Religion*, vol. 12, pp. 217–18.

REVIEWS

5. W. Thesiger, *The Life of My Choice* in *Times Literary Supplement*, 4 September, pp. 941–2.
6. J. Alpher, ed., *Nationalism and Modernity* in *International Affairs*, vol. 63, pp. 299–300.
7. W. Cleveland, *Islam against the West*, in *Bulletin of the School of Oriental and African Studies*, vol. 50, pp. 555–6.
8. S. O. Carré et G. Michaud, *Les Frères Musulmans* and G. Kepel, *Le Prophète et Pharaon* in *Maghreb Review*, vol. 10, pp. 118–19.

1988

BOOK

1. [Advisory Ed.] *Cambridge Encyclopedia of the Middle East and North Africa*. (Cambridge, Cambridge University Press, 504 **pp**.

PAMPHLET

2. *The Middle East Centre, 1957–1987: A Short History*. Oxford. St Antony's College, 17 pp.

ARTICLES

3. 'Religion', 'Education', 'Christians in the Muslim period' and 'History of the Middle East since 1939' in 1988, entry 1, pp. 32–7, 139–43, 190–5 and 277–9.
4. 'Musa 'Alami and the Problem of Palestine, 1933–49' in H. Nashabe, ed., *Studia Palaestina: Studies in Honour of Constantine Zurayk*. Beirut, Institute of Palestine Studies, pp. 23–41.
5. 'Conclusion' in J. A. Bill and W. R. Louis, eds, *Musaddiq, Iranian Nationalism and Oil*. London, I.B.Tauris, pp. 329–40.
6. 'Visions of Lebanon' in Halim Barakat, ed., *Towards a Viable Lebanon*. London, Croom Helm (in association with the Center for Contemporary Arab Studies, Georgetown University), pp. 3–14.
7. 'Foreword' to P. Partner, *Arab Voices*. London, British Broadcasting Corporation, pp. vi–vii.
8. 'Elizabeth Monroe' in *St Antony's College Record 1985–1989*, pp. 139–44. [Reprint of 1986, entry 2]
9. 'Wednesday afternoons remembered' in *Fi Sirat Jamal* (Memorial volume for Jamal Mohammad Ahmed). University of Khartoum Press, pp. I27–40.

REVIEWS

10. A. A. Duri, *The Historical Formation of the Arab Nation* in *Middle East International*, 3 January, pp. 22–3.
11. A. Popovic and G. Veinstein, *Les ordres mystiques dans l'islam* in *Maghreb Review*, vol. 13, pp. 122–23.

12. M. Johnson, *Class and Client in Beirut* in *Bulletin of the School of Oriental and African Studies,* vol. 51, pp. 336.
13. P. M. Holt and M. W. Daly, *A History of the Sudan* in *Bulletin of the School of Oriental and African Studies,* vol. 51, p. 620.
14. R. Simon, *Ignaz Goldziher* in *Bulletin of the British Society for Middle Eastern Studies,* vol. 15 (i and ii), 140–1.

1989

ARTICLES

1. 'Foreword' to R. S. Abujaber, *Pioneers over Jordan.* London, I.B.Tauris, pp. xi–xii.
2. 'Foreword' to G. Grant, *Middle Eastern Photographic Collections in the United Kingdom.* Durham, Middle East Libraries Committee, p. v.
3. 'Foreword' to K. Tidrick, *Heart-Beguiling Araby.* London, I.B.Tauris, pp. xiii–xvi.
4. 'Conclusion' in W. R. Louis and R. Owen, eds. *Suez 1956: The Crisis and its Consequences.* Oxford, Clarendon Press, pp. 393–410.
5. 'L'encyclopédie de Bustani' in *Rivages et déserts: hommage à Jacques Berque.* Paris, Sindbad, pp. 197–208.
6. 'In Memoriam: Martin Hinds' in *Bulletin of the Middle East Studies Association of North America,* vol. 13, pp. 140–1.
7. 'Samuel Stern' in *Memorial Addresses of All Souls College.* Oxford, All Souls College (for private circulation), pp. 73–6 [Reprint of 1970, entry 6]

REVIEWS

8. R. Betts, *The Druze* in *The Tablet,* 10 June, pp. 671–2.
9. R. Simon, *Ignaz Goldziher: His Life and Scholarship as Reflected in his Works and Correspondence* in *Bulletin of the British Society for Middle Eastern Studies,* vol. 15, pp. 140–1.

1990

ARTICLE

1. 'Bustani's Encyclopaedia' in *Journal of Islamic Studies* (Oxford), vol. 1, pp. 111–19. [English version of 1983, entry 5]

2. 'The Arab Awakening forty years after' in D. Hopwood, ed. *Studies in Arab History*. London, Macmillan, pp. 21–40. [Reprint of chapter 13 in 1981, entry 1]
3. 'Islam in European Thought' in G. B. Peterson, ed. *The Tannner Lectures on Human Values: XI 1990*. Salt Lake City, University of Utah Press, pp. 223–87.

REVIEWS

4. R. Fisk, *Pity the Nation* and A. Oz, *The Slopes of Lebanon* in *The Times Literary Supplement*, 2 March, pp. 219–20.
5. J. Wilson, *Lawrence of Arabia* in *The Independent on Sunday*, 19 January, p. 22.
6. A. B. Gaunson, *The Anglo-French Clash in Lebanon and Syria* in *English Historical Review*, vol. 105, pp. 261–2.
7. T. Philipp, *The Syrians in Egypt 1729–1925* in *Journal of Islamic Studies*, vol. 1, pp.167–9.
8. P. Mansfield, *Kuwait: Vanguard of the Gulf* in *The Tablet*, 6 October, p. 1276.
9. S. R. Sonyel, *The Ottoman Armenians* in *English Historical Review*, vol. 105, pp. 1073–4.

1991

BOOKS

1. *A History of the Arab Peoples*. London, Faber/Cambridge (MA), The Belknap Press of Harvard University Press, 551 pp.
2. *Islam in European Thought*. Cambridge, Cambridge University Press. [Includes, with revisions: 1977, entry 1; 1978, entry 3; 1980, entry 3; 1982, entry 1; 1983, entry 2; 1988, entry 3; 1990, entries 1 and 3; 1991, entry 3]

ARTICLES

3. 'How Should We Write the History of the Middle East?' in *International Journal of Middle East Studies*, vol. 23, pp. 125–36.
4. 'L'oeuvre d'André Raymond' in *Revue du Monde Musulman et de la Méditerranée*, 55/56, pp. 18–27.

5. 'The Achievement of André Raymond', translation of 'L'oeuvre d'André Raymond' in *British Journal of Middle Eastern Studies*, vol. 18 (I) 5–15.
6. 'Sulayman al-Bustani (1856–1925)' in S. Seikaly, R. Baalbaki and P. Dodd, eds, *Quest for Understanding: Arabic and Islamic Studies in Memory of Malcolm H. Kerr*. Beirut, American University of Beirut Press, pp. 43–97.
7. 'In Memory of Malcolm Kerr' and 'Conclusion: Tribes and States in Islamic History' in P. Khoury and J. Kostiner, eds, *Tribes and State Formation in the Middle East*, University of California Press and London, I.B.Tauris, pp. xi–xiii, and 303–11.
8. 'Foreword' in R. A. Fernea and W. R. Louis, eds, *The Iraqi Revolution of 1958*. London, I.B.Tauris, pp.vii–viii.
9. Autobiographical essay, unpublished.

REVIEW

10. K. Kyle, *Suez* in *Daily Telegraphy*, 6 July, p. xxvi.

1992

BOOK

1. [Ed. with Nadim Shehadi] *The Lebanese in the World: A Century of Emigration*. London, The Centre for Lebanese Studies in association with I.B.Tauris & Co Ltd.

ARTICLES

2. 'Introduction' and 'Egypt' in Hourani and N. Shehadi, eds, *The Lebanese in the World*. London, The Centre for Lebanese Studies in association with I.B.Tauris & Co Ltd.
3. 'Introduction' in N. Rose (ed.) *From Palmerston to Balfour: Collected Essays of Mayir Vereté*. London: Frank Cass, pp. viii–xiv.
4. 'Foreword' in W. Khalidi, *Palestine Reborn*. London: I.B.Tauris, pp. ix–xii.

Index

'Abduh, Muhammad, 81, 83, 93–5
Abdülhamid II, Sultan, 66, 71
Acre, 59
Aden, 36
Afghan, 94
Afghani, Jamal al-Din al-, 31n, 83, 92–5
Ahmed, Jamal Muhammad, 26
Ajami, Fouad, 98–9, 149
'Akkar, 146
Alami, Musa, 25, 111–12, 117, 124
Albanians, 64, 73
Aleppo, 51, 87, 100, 164
Alexandria, 79, 155, 179
Algeria, 65
Ali, Muhammad, 67–8
America/American, 12, 16, 18, 37–9, 45, 61, 86–7, 98, 112, 114, 117, 121, 123, 137, 153, 174; *see also under* United States
American University of Beirut, 17, 21, 26, 36, 78, 107, 129
Anglo-American Committee of Inquiry, 15, 25, 115–16, 121, 123, 139, 125
Annales school, 33–4, 39, 43
Antonius, George, 3, 9, 21, 72, 77–80, 90, 98, 103, 166, 178
Arab/Arabs, 1–4, 6–14, 20–6, 28, 30–1, 36, 39–40, 42, 45, 47–9, 50–2, 54–5, 57–8, 60, 64–5, 67–8, 70–5, 77–84, 89–93, 95–101, 103–6, 108–12, 115–28, 138–40, 142, 145, 149, 151–9, 161–71, 173–4, 176–9
Arab League, 3, 73, 110, 121–2
Arab nationalism, 3–4, 10–14, 15–16, 21, 39, 77–9, 82–3, 89–102, 104–5, 107, 137–43, 152, 164–7, 169–71
Arab Office, 3, 6, 25, 110–12, 115–16, 122–3, 127
Arab rebellion, 20, 107–8, 124
Arab revolt, 73, 95
Arabia, 50, 155
Arabian Peninsula, 8, 12, 96,

176
Arabic, 17, 42, 49, 54, 71, 84, 90, 155, 173
Arabism/pan-Arabism, 43, 70–2, 80, 90, 97–100, 102, 104, 111
Arafat, Yasir, 153
Arqoub, 132
Armenians, 64
Asia/Asian, 37, 40, 52–3, 147, 164; *see also* Central Asia
Astor, David, 126n
Atlantic, 3, 39–40, 115
Avicenna, *see under* Ibn Sina

Ba'th Party, 102
Baghdad, 17, 40, 59–60
Balfour Declaration, 110
Baroja, J. C., 146
Baudelaire, Charles, 106, 127
Beirut, 14, 17, 22, 107, 129, 134, 136, 138, 144–5, 148–50, 158, 178
Ben Gurion, David, 23
Berkeley, 55n
Berque, Jacques, 34, 159, 174
Bethlehem, 86
Bilad al-Sham, 134
Biqa', 146
Bowen, Harold, 28, 48
Brazil, 14
Britain, 3, 14, 22, 27–8, 37, 64, 77, 80, 85–6, 96, 103, 108, 110–11, 121, 123–5, 127, 136, 157, 171–3, 178
British Mandate, 20
Bulgarians, 64

Byzantines, 45
Byzantium, 58

Cairo, 2, 8, 17, 23–4, 40, 47, 49, 51, 59–60, 65, 67–9, 87, 95, 155, 163
Central Asia, 64
Centre for Lebanese Studies, Oxford, 158n, 159
Chatham House, 22
Chicago, University of, 33, 38, 40
Christ, 172
Christian(s), 1, 10, 12, 14, 24, 30, 50, 64, 68, 70, 77, 81, 83–93, 96–7, 129, 136, 138, 142–3, 146, 148, 152, 164, 166, 172
Christendom, 142
Christianity, 113, 149, 171–2
Church of England, 19
Church of the Holy Nativity, 86
Church of the Holy Sepulchre, 86
Clayton, Brigadier I. N., 23
communism, 81, 173–4
Constantinople, 51; *see also* Istanbul
Copts, 91
Crimean War, 86
Crum, Bartley, 121

Damascus, 17, 51, 71–2, 87, 136, 164
Dartmouth College, 38
Dawn, C. Ernest, 30, 71–2

Index

Dayr al-Qamar, 79, 148
de Gaulle, Charles, 150
Descartes, René, 20
Didsbury Preparatory School, 19
Din II, Fakhr al-, 134, 147
Druze, 134, 136, 138, 143, 146–8, 170

Egypt/Egyptian, 7, 17, 34, 51, 59, 65, 68, 73, 83, 91, 93–4, 96–8, 100, 163
England, 3, 12–13, 16, 18–19, 21, 79, 81, 112, 129, 158–9, 167, 169, 172
Enlightenment, 66
Europe, 7, 31, 37–8, 45, 52–3, 61, 63–4, 66–8, 70, 83, 86, 89, 91–2, 95, 97, 112, 115–16, 121, 167, 172–3, 175–6

Faisal, Emir, 123
Fascist, 116
Fawaz, Leila, 5
Fertile Crescent, 8, 42, 47–8, 60, 65, 68–9, 83, 87, 89, 97–8, 170, 176
First World War, 50, 78, 80, 96, 107, 137, 164, 166
Foreign Office, 6, 11, 108, 110, 132, 156
Foreign Office Research Department, 2, 108, 132
France, 64, 67, 80–1, 85–6, 96, 136–8, 141, 171

French Revolution, 7

Gaza, 126, 169
German Romantics, 100–1
Germany, 37, 111
Gibb, H. A. R., 22–3, 26, 28, 36–8, 41, 44, 48
Gladstone, Mr W. E., 158
Glubb Pasha, 23
Göttingen, University of, 100
Granada, 155
Greater Lebanon, 18, 137–8, 141, 148
Greater Syria, 96–7, 116, 139–40
Greek(s), 63, 138
Greek Orthodox Church, 17, 79, 90, 138
Gulf, 8, 42, 60
Gulf War, 157

Haim, Sylvia, 90, 91
Hamidian policy, 71
Hanbal, Ahmad Ibn, 153
Harvard, 21, 36, 38, 41
Hasbaya, 132
Hashemites, 95
Hauran, 16
Hayter Committee, 37–8
Hebrew, 115
Hermon, Mount, 131
Hijaz, 51, 59
Hitti, Philip, 20
Hobbesian, 52, 74
Hodgson, Marshall, 40, 174
Holocaust, 114
Hopwood, Derek, 158–9

Hourani, Cecil, 5, 18, 111–12, 122–3, 130–2
Hourani, Fadlo, 16–20, 130
Hourani, George, 19
Hourani, Susanna, 27
Husayn, Sharif, 95
Hussein, Saddam, 105, 153
Husseini, Hajj Amin, 121
Husri, Sati al-, 100–2
Hutcheson, Judge Joe, 139

India, 64, 94
Indian Ocean, 42, 61
Iran, 93–4, 151
Iraq/Iraqi(s), 8, 11, 77, 95–6, 100–2, 110, 153, 166, 170
Islam/Islamic, 1, 8–10, 20, 27–9, 31, 34–6, 40, 42–5, 49–54, 58–60, 62, 69–72, 75, 81–4, 87–95, 104, 113, 134, 137, 140, 146, 149, 159–61, 171–4, 176–7
Ismailism, 51
Israel/Israeli, 16, 25, 100, 125–6, 151, 154, 168–9
Issawi, Charles, 27, 122n, 175, 177
Istanbul, 17, 43, 49–50, 58, 60, 65, 67–9, 71, 73, 74, 163, 166; *see also* Constantinople
Italian, 65

Jabal Amil, 134
Janissary regiments, 66
Jansen, G. H., 15

Jerusalem, 15, 25, 86–7, 110–11, 121, 155
Jesus, 172; *see also* Christ
Jews/Jewish, 17, 19–20, 64, 68, 70, 84, 87, 97, 106, 108–9, 121, 124–5, 169; Judaism, 113
Jidda, 87
Jordan, 126

Kant, Immanuel, 20
Keddie, Nikki, 31
Kedourie, Elie, 31–2, 72, 90, 168–9
Khaldun, Ibn, 40, 74, 153, 155
Khazin family, 148
Khoury, Philip, 71–2
Kisrawan, 136, 148
Kramer, Martin, 156–7, 175
Kurds, 64, 73
Kuwait, 77, 105

Labour government, 116
Lapidus, Ira, 55–6
Lawrence, T. E., 21–2, 78–9, 89, 164
Lebanon, 8, 11, 13–14, 16, 18–19, 21, 59, 79, 84, 87, 91, 96–7, 105, 108, 129–30, 132–52, 166, 170, 176
Leo X, 147
Levant, 91, 176
Lewis, Bernard, 33, 62
Liberal Party, 19

Index

Libya, 65
Locke, John, 20
London, 3, 6, 19–20, 22, 41
London, University of, 41, 110

Ma'n dynasty, 134
Maans, 145
Magdalen College, Oxford, 19, 26, 36
Maghrib, 42
Malik, Charles, 21
Mamluk, 55, 59, 57, 148
Manchester, 1, 11, 16–20, 105, 130–31, 158
Marçais, Georges and William, 53
Mardin, Serif, 67
Marjayoun, 16–18, 105, 127, 130–2
Maronite, 14, 97, 134–8, 141–4, 146–7, 149, 170
Marxism, 33–4, 154
Massignon, Louis, 41, 79, 89, 174
Mecca, 95, 155–6
Mediterranean, 42, 61, 97, 105, 129, 145, 176
Middle East(ern), 1–7, 9, 12, 16, 18–24, 26–8, 30, 35–8, 43–5, 47, 49, 62–3, 74, 76–7, 82, 86, 93, 103, 112, 116, 130, 132, 136, 147, 158, 167–8, 170–2, 175
Middle East Centre, 36–8, 41
Mill, John Stuart, 20
Mill Hill, 19

Monroe, Elizabeth, 3, 37
Morocco, 12, 17, 50
Mosul, 59, 87, 164
Mount Lebanon, 14, 87, 134–6, 143, 148
Muhammad, Prophet, 171–2
Muslims, 2, 4, 7, 9–10, 12, 14, 30, 35, 40, 50–1, 53, 55–6, 58, 63–4, 68–9, 71–2, 83–4, 87–9, 91–5, 136–8, 142, 144, 146–7, 153, 155, 166, 168, 172

Nablus, 87, 164
Napoleon Bonaparte, 7
Nasir, Jamal 'Abd al-, 26, 97–8, 100, 143; Nasirism, 98
National Pact, 141–3
Nazi, 111, 116
Near East, 18, 53, 64, 84–5
Niebuhr, Reinhold, 174–5
Nile, 40
North Africa, 8, 17, 153, 163
notables, 2, 39, 50, 55–60, 65, 68–72, 74, 78, 87, 97, 160–4, 168

Ottoman(s), 1, 9, 12, 39, 43, 47–50, 52, 54–6, 58–67, 70, 72–6, 83–6, 88, 90, 95–6, 99–100, 134–7, 144, 148, 162–6, 179; Ottoman Empire, 17, 24, 28, 38, 48, 49–42, 61–1, 65, 72, 74–5,

83–6, 88, 99, 138, 144, 164; Ottomanism/Ottomanists, 70–2, 100, 165; Young Ottomans, 66
Owen, Roger, 157–8, 177
Oxford, 1, 12, 15, 19–21, 26, 34, 36–9, 41, 123, 157–8, 178
Oxus, 40

Pacific, 40
Palestine, 2–4, 6–7, 10–11, 13, 15, 20–1, 24–5, 59, 77, 80, 97, 100, 106–12, 114–15, 127–8, 156, 166, 168–9, 173; Palestinian(s), 2–3, 10–11, 13, 20, 25, 107, 109–12, 115, 121, 124–7, 151, 168–70
Palestine Liberation Organization, 153
Pennsylvania, University of, 38
Persia/Persian, 54, 59–60, 73, 83, 93
Phalanges, 148
Pipes, Daniel, 153–6, 175
Porte, 59, 62, 85, 87
Presbyterian Church, 17–18
Protestant(ism), 17, 27, 85, 87
Public Record Office, 28

Racy, Soumaya, 16–17
Raymond, André, 26, 34–5, 53, 75
Red Sea, 68

Reid, Donald, xv, 30, 32, 77, 79
Romanians, 64
Royal Institute of International Affairs (RIIA), 22, 28, 132
Russia/Russian, 37, 64, 85–6, 123

Sa'ada, Antun, 96–7, 139–40
Said, Nuri al-, 110
St Antony's College, 36–7
Salibi, Kamal, 143–4
Sasanians, 45
Sa'ud, 'Abd al-'Aziz Ibn 'Abd al-Rahman al-, *see* Saud, Ibn
Saud, Ibn, 176
Sayda, xxiv, 18, 134, 144
School of Oriental and African Studies, 41
Second World War, 2–3, 22, 132, 141
Semites, 164
Serbs, 63
Sharabi, Hisham, 30
Shi'i/Shi'ism, 51, 59, 94, 134, 138, 141, 143, 146, 170
Shihab dynasty, 134–5, 145, 150
Shuf mountains, 79
Shuqairi, Ahmed, 117
Sina, Ibn, 153
Six-Day War, 98–9, 125–6, 169
Souk al Khan, 132
Spain, 155

Stern, Samuel, 41
Sudan/Sudanese, 17, 26
Suez crisis, 36
Sunni(s), 94, 134, 138, 141–4, 146–7, 149, 170
Surrey University, 27
Syria/Syrian, 8, 11, 16–19, 21–2, 51, 59–60, 68–71, 84, 89, 95–7, 100–2, 107, 134, 138–40, 151, 153, 166, 170, 176
Syrian Social Nationalist Party, 96, 139

Talmon, J. L., 125, 126n
Tanzimat, 56, 62–3, 88
Texas, 107
Tibi, Bassam, 100–2
Toynbee, Arnold, 22, 28–9, 40, 103–4
Transjordan, 166
Tripoli, 14, 134, 138, 144
Tunis, 155
Tunisia, 65
Turkey, 8, 62, 86, 93–4
Turks/Turkish, 45, 49, 51, 54, 64, 66, 70, 72–3, 86, 93, 164–5, 167

'ulama, 28, 54–5, 59, 59, 72, 160–2
Umayyad caliphate, 140
United Nations, 112, 121
United Nations, General Assembly of the, 122
United Nations Special Committee on Palestine (UNSCOP), 121
United States, 27, 37–8, 112, 114–16, 143; *see also under* America/American

Victoria College, 79

Wadi Teym, 132
Washington, 33, 110–11
Weber, Max, 20, 53, 161
Wegg-Prosser, Odile, 27
Wendell, Charles, 30
West Bank, 126, 169
Wilson, Edmund, 30

Yishuv, 20
Young Turks, 72

Zahla, 148
Zionism/Zionist, 2, 10–11, 13, 25, 107–14, 117–19, 121–7, 168–70
Zurayq, Qustantin, 21